BEAUTIFULLY BROKEN

How God Restored This Broken Vessel and Made Me Whole

by Angela Kelly

Published by Threepeppers Publishing

1st Edition – March 2024

ISBN: 9781838494384

Cover:
The Broken Vessel
Drawing © Angela Kelly

www.3peppers.co.uk

To the people I love

DISCLAIMER

This is my autobiographical writing, based on my journey toward repentance, forgiveness, and redemption. The content of this book consists of my life in Jamaica and my emigration to England. The information in this book represents the people who have impacted my life in one form or another and have been instrumental in my journey from birth to adulthood; and finally catapulting my life to acknowledging Christ Jesus as my Lord and Saviour, who has taken me through unforgiveness, to forgiveness, and repentance, to freedom in Christ, without whom this book would never be written.

I know that not everyone will accept my views and opinions, or my version of the truth, but I hope that by writing my story, it will go some way towards helping anyone who may find themselves in a similar situation.

Along the way, I have come to realise that God does not take us out of our trials, He takes us through them so that we can learn some valuable lessons along the way. In fact, He uses the scrapes that we get ourselves into, through our disobedience, to create his greatest masterpiece. Make no mistake about this, God is all-seeing, all-knowing, all-consuming, all-powerful God; if we never worshiped Him, He would still Be. Because He lives outside of the created space and time, in what is referred to as the Everlasting Now. In other words, He lives in the past, present and our future. All at once He is ever present in all our tomorrows, He knows all about the mistakes we make, as we navigate our way through life's trials and storms. He knows about the raging battles without and within, confronting us daily, that is why He has gone ahead for an answer. He will always be perfectly glorious, perfectly loving, and wonderfully God, who never changes; He is the same yesterday today and forever. He is no respecter of persons.

So, I hope that by charting my struggles through life, I can help someone, who is on the verge of making those same mistakes, to get closure. It is important that we learn from life's hard knocks because God loves us too much to allow us to continue climbing up and down the same old mountain over and over again. Similarly, when we train our own children, we set out the rules and pitfalls, to protect them and keep them safe.

God does the same for us. He chastens us for our own good. The Bible says, "if He chases us we are Sons, and if He doesn't, we are legitimate. (Hebrews 12:5-11) and "though you slay me I will still praise you." (Job 13:15)

Through it all, I did not know that I was God's Masterpiece in the making. However, I had to tell the truth and expose the lies. Thus, shaming the devil.

DEDICATION

This book is dedicated to my Lord and Saviour Jesus Christ. I thank you Lord for where you have taken me from, where I am today, and where you are about to take me. It has been the ride of my life. Thank you for not hiding away from my mess but helping me to clean it up. I could not have done it without you. The Bible says: "Except the Lord builds our house, we labour in vain... (Psalm 127:1). Thank you for building a secure fence around me and mine, protecting me from the devil's wicked darts, and most of all, thank you for lifting me up from the "miry clay" (Psalm 40:2) and setting my feet upon the rock to stay. The Bible says, "When a man's ways please the Lord he makes even his enemies live at peace with him." (Proverbs 16:7). So I thank you Lord for giving me peace in the middle of my storm.

FOREWORD

I did not like my reflection. I did not think I looked aesthetically pleasing at all. I came to the realisation that I did not love myself enough. I remember looking in the mirror and not liking what I was seeing. I thought that my nose was too big, my lips too thick and my eyes looked like cats' eyes. In fact, I was frightened to look in the mirror. So, for a time, I just stopped looking. When I examined the reason why I felt like that about myself, I realised that these were the areas that my mom criticised me in, which in turn led me down a path of self-loathing. Then the Lord began to work on my self-esteem. He told me to look in the mirror each day, confess self-love, and know that He loves me, just as I am, because He chose me before time began. Man, only sees the outward appearance, but God sees beyond the outward. Therefore, we must love ourselves; if we don't have self-love, how can we give love, or how can we accept the love of others? We must allow God to build us up from the inside out, and trust in the process. Because if you don't believe in your own beauty, then no one will, and it doesn't matter who tells you that you are beautiful, you will find it hard to accept. Most importantly God did not reject anything that He made. "Everything He made He said was 'good'" (Genesis 1:31). It took years of being moulded and reshaped by God, for me to truly believe this. In addition, when you don't have self-love, there is a spirit that follows you, which makes some people around you see in you, what you see in yourself. But when you have self-confidence, it's a beautiful and attractive thing to behold. When people see your confidence, they react to you accordantly. However, we are all in God's beauty shop.

Some come, dear readers, come and drink from the fountain of eternal life. God is going to heal you wherever you hurt; don't leave it too late, He is coming back soon.

I'd like to quote this passage from Bob and Debby Gas in its entirety. "When you don't feel good about yourself, you live with a sense of insecurity. You keep looking to others for validation or approval, and when you don't get it, your sense of worth shrivels. As a result, you can spend your life living far short of your God - given potential. You are the only person you can't get away from, and until you learn to accept yourself based on the fact that God loves and accepts you as you are, you will always battle insecurities. Think about the last time you were around somebody you didn't particularly enjoy. How did it make you feel? Not good, right? Good or bad, we project onto others the thoughts and feelings we have about ourselves. So, if you want people to think well of you, you must have a good opinion of yourself-based on God's word. Now, the Bible does warn us about having an over-inflated opinion of ourselves. However, don't go to the other extreme. Living in continual self-rejection is an open invitation to Satan, who, the Bible says is going around like a roaring Lion seeking someone he may devour." (Gass, 2024). Know this: the good qualities you do possess are evidence that God is at work in your life.

Psalm 139 is like a love story to me and to you from the Lord: "I will praise thee for I am fearfully and wonderfully made; marvellous are thy works; and that my soul knows right well" (Psalm 139:14). He also said that He knew me/you from before I/you was formed in my/your mother's womb, He knew me/you by name [...] and his thoughts are precious, towards me/you. In addition, I/we are made in the image and likeness of God, so, when He made me/us, He said it was good. So, because I know that God's word, is true, who am I to say any diffident.

Most importantly, "you can't hide it from God" (Hebrews 4:13-15).

Contents

INTRODUCTION: Origins

I am 66 years old, and my name is Angela Kelly. I was born on the beautiful Caribbean Island of Jamaica, in Kingston Town, to Mavis Summer and Stanley Anderson. I don't remember anything about my father. My parents split up when I was very young while still living in Jamaica. When I was 3 years old, and my sister was months-old, my mom left us with our aunt Florie, and travelled to England, to look for a better life. Prior to this, my mom met a man on the island, who expressed great interest in her, by the name of James Smith. After getting to know him, she realized that he was sincere in his feelings for her, and she in turn reciprocated her feelings for him. After emigrating to England, James Smith later filed for Mom, who came over in the early 1960s. They got married and went to have 5 more children. In total mom had 7 children.

Mom left my sister and I with our Aunty Florie in Jamaica for a while, so that she could look for work in England, and be able to eventually send for us. However, possibly a year later, our Aunty also received an offer to immigrate to England, which meant she had to leave us with other people. Notably, she left my sister and I with my sister's father and his family (not my father), telling mom that he was happy to take us in and that he is a very nice man, but mom did not approve of this turn of events, but it was out of her hands. It appears that there was no other option. For me, that was the beginning of a nightmare, I thought would never end.

We were mistreated from the beginning. I especially suffered greatly at the hands of my sister's stepsister (not mine). I went through a great deal of abuse in Jamaica. Many years had passed after auntie left us. Finally, news reached my mother about the mistreatment we were experiencing, especially when she found out that I was sexually abused, so she proceeded as quickly as she could, to lodge an application for me to come to England for me. Mom later sent for my sister, but she was not ready to come yet. I believe she was in a relationship at the time. But I missed my sister so much because we were very close. It felt like a part of me was missing for a long time. When everyone would gang up against me, I used to wish that my sister was there to stand up to them with me.

It was years later, when my sister was in her early thirties, with two children of her own, John and Julian, that she expressed a desire to come to England, so Mom filed for her. When she settled in England, she in turn sent for her two children. So, now all Mrs Summer's children are now with her in England.

Upon my arrival in England, I met my new brothers and sisters. I was very happy to meet them. After attending both primary and secondary school in England, I went to college, then university, to further my education.

CHAPTER I: Time spent with Auntie Florie and Uncle Victor

When I came to England, I met up with my aunt Florie again, who lived in the beautiful, picturesque town of Wellingborough, Northamptonshire, where she lived with her male partner, uncle Vic. We lived in a two-bedroom council house, and I had my own room, which was a novelty to me. I remember having lots of toys to play with. Out of them all, I remember a doll that Auntie gave me; she named her Wendy. I loved Wendy so much. I used to love changing her into a new set of clothes every day. Not having to share anything was a bonus, but the only trouble was that it was lonely playing all by myself. In hindsight, had I stayed in Wellingborough with my Auntie, I would have been far better off because the school friends I made there were far more genuine than those in London, but I was also missing my brothers and sisters, and longing for my mom to change towards me and show me some love, the way I believed she should.

So, I would alternate between my mom and my aunt, between London school and Wellingborough school, which I preferred far more because the teachers were a lot more caring and encouraging., Yet, my mom wasn't there, so I would spend the school holidays with my aunt, and sometimes I would spend the whole year with her. My aunt worked at a women's old people's home, and she would sometimes take me to work with her. I was between 9 and 10 years old at the time, and I would be given treats, like biscuits, cakes, crisps, and sweets, from the people auntie took care of. They treated me with love and kindness, and generally fussed over me. They would let me sit on their lap and bounce me up and down. As a child starved of affection, oh, I loved the attention, but they weren't mum, were they? In those days, aunties, grandmas, female relatives and close family female friends would take care of the child so that the parents could work. They would take the place of a foster carer/childminder. Sometimes the child would become a permanent fixture in the adopted household. Proving the saying, it truly takes a village to raise a child, so that the child can benefit from the lived experience of some colourful characters, as the child tries to navigate their way through the complexities of life.

Looking back at life with Auntie Florie. it was very good. It was a very special time for me because I felt loved. I remember some special times. As a little girl, she used to let me play with her soft wrinkly neck and she would laugh as it tickled. When I dared to try it with mum (I am smiling a little now), she just pushed me away. That was obviously not her thing! But having my own space to grow up in, with auntie, was still a welcomed freedom. I had my doll Wendy for company, who I could talk to as if she was a real person. In other words, she replaced my siblings, who lived in London.

However, when I eventually left Wellingborough to settle down in London, I remembered asking my aunt if I could take my doll Wendy with me, but she said no. 'When you come to spend time with me again she will be here,' she said, but I suspect aunty was more attached to Wendy than she was letting on, because years later, when she was over ninety years old, and about to die, mom said it was as if her spirit went into Wendy, and as auntie closed her eyes, so did Wendy.

Although for the most part I enjoyed living with my aunt and uncle Vic, I didn't always like the way she treated him. She was always picking arguments and fights with him over one thing or another, especially over money, and she would sometimes chase him down with the broom stick, and call him a miser. She would steal his money, which he hid under the floor boards. She would take money out a little at a time so that he didn't notice, but one day he caught her lifting up the floorboards. She couldn't believe that he came home early from work and caught her stealing his money. They ended up having the master of all rows, with auntie winning as usual. I felt like I was watching a movie; they tore into each other, like they were in a bull ring, with auntie always winning, leaving uncle feeling as If he was the one in the wrong. Despite all this, he still loved and respected her. She, on the other hand, was in love with another man. But I would try to stick up for Uncle Vic, because he was always good to me.

In those early days, black people didn't have easy access to banks, so they developed a system called a partnership, where there is a banker, who keeps the money, and the saver, who entrust the banker with their money. Although there was no interest, it enabled us to save up for big events and important occasions. Because we could not withdraw money as and when, like other banks, it meant we had to wait until it was our time to withdraw. Not that Uncle Victor would use a bank anyway. It would sometimes make me laugh at their antics, but I sometimes felt Uncle Vic's pain.

Back in London, life had its challenges, living with my brothers and sisters. All six of us had to share one bed, but we still had some fun times. In those days, we occupied only two rooms, one for mom and dad, and one for us, because they had to rent out the other four rooms in order to pay the mortgage.

CHAPTER II: My road to adulthood

My road to adulthood was full of ups and downs. Mom and I had similar temperaments, so we often clashed, and then I would clash with my siblings, especially with my younger sister Edna. Mom could never see my side of things. She never gave my siblings any boundaries where I was concerned, and when mom and I disagreed about something, she would get my brothers and sisters on her side, so I never felt respected by my younger siblings. This was hard to take, because in Jamaican culture the eldest sibling was always looked up to. I just felt like the black sheep of the family. When I left home at an early age, I went through a lot of suffering and heart ache, out there on my own. I had been hurt so much, over a long period of time, starting from Jamaica, and I thought the only way to move and push past my pain, was to treat well the people who treated me bad, and put it out of my mind, forget it, and start over again; and that is what I did. If anyone hurt me, I would try to forgive them while still feeling the pain, let it fester for a while, and then keep it down, and still continue with that person, as if nothing ever happened. However, trying to do so without knowing God, is a very hard task. You become like a pressure cooker, a volcano waiting to erupt at the slightest provocation, so unbeknownst to me I harboured a lot of unforgiveness, resentment, leading to feelings of abandonment, which I suffered through rejection. But what the devil meant for my detriment; God turned it around for my betterment.

Little did I realize at that time, that all that I went through, put in God's hand, was to become the making of my character. The Lord started me on a journey of healing, self-improvement, and restoration, that had begun through life's hard knocks, and ultimately, academic achievements. The Bible says, "My people are destroyed for lack of knowledge, sometimes we don't know the freedom we could have in Christ" (Hosea 4:6). I enjoyed my school, and college life, but I went through days of underachievement, before finally achieving all of which did help me acquire some of the essential tools, enabling me to move forward in life to date. I had an all-around good education. It started late, but I worked hard to catch up, but I did not know how to correctly apply my knowledge. It wasn't until I was in my early thirties, when I got into Polytechnic and then University, that my life began to make some sense. Among my passions was reading. I became good at English, Art, and History. My first job was also a key, part of the educational process. Through it all God taught me to forgive those who hurt me, used and abused me. I would bless, and pray for them so that the Lord could work on me. The problem with a lot of us is that, when we fall down, we fail to get up again. Failure is all part of the learning process. The saying goes. it is not how you start; it is how you finish. I thank God for this saying.

Because it has helped me get up many times in my life, what does it mean to forgive? People often say, 'I can forgive, but I won't forget,' but they are merely fooling themselves, because when you truly forgive, you also truly forget. Then the heart can be healed. The only true path to salvation and redemption is to accept Jesus Christ as your Lord and Saviour, and He will teach you how to forgive and forget. But know this, the act of forgiveness is a faith move; you must believe and apply God's word, and it will happen over time. It is a process. So, if anyone tells you that they can forgive, but they won't forget, that person is holding onto unforgiveness. In addition, when you have truly forgiven, you will no longer feel the pain in the pit of your stomach, tugging at your heart strings. So, don't let unforgiveness infiltrate your heart and turn it to stone. If you don't forgive, you are only harming yourself.

So, quite simply, my message to my readers is to forgive and be made whole. Because "you can't hide it from God" (Hebrews 4:13-15).

The English Dictionary defines "unforgiveness" as a person blaming another for wrong or perceived wrong done to them. It brings feelings of anger, leading to rage, resentment, and bitterness, and a whole lot of other complications. Negative and destructive emotions emerge. Saying to yourself I can't forgive, or I will never forgive, is not an option in the grand scheme of things, because with God's help you can. The Word says, "I can do all things through Christ who strengthens me" (Philippians 4:13).

Jesus rates forgiveness as very high on his list of priorities. I have found there to be roughly twenty-eight scriptures on forgiveness in the

Bible. Most important of all, when Peter was fed up with being hurt by his brethren, he went to Jesus and asked him how many times he should forgive his brother. Is it seven times seven? Jesus replied, "I say not unto thee, Until seven times: but, Until seventy times seven" (Matthew, 18:22).

In other words, infinite. The Lord knows that an unforgiving heart is the devil's playground. So, if I wanted to be made whole, I had to make a conscious decision to forgive all those who wronged me, and those people were sometimes the closest to me. Let's face it: you will rarely need to forgive an acquaintance, because if you don't let them get close enough to hurt you, the devil will use the people to whom you have given your heart to, to do you harm. No matter how much someone has hurt you, you have to forgive them; not for their sake, but for yours, because when they hurt you, they have power over you, and when you don't forgive, they keep the power. And then you forgive yourself.

I have selected a few scriptures on forgiveness, to use as examples and clarify my point. Forgiving those who trespass against you, is one of the key ingredients to our overall wellbeing. The Word says "To whom you forgive anything God also forgive you. For if I forgive anything, to whom I forgive, I forgive it for your sake" (2 Corinthians 2:10). Furthermore, "when we confess our sins, He is faithful and just to forgive us our transgressions, and to clean us from all unrighteousness" (1 John 1:9).

My experience almost mirrors the Minister and Author Joyce Meyer's experience. I am using extracts from her work to convey some of my deepest anguish.

She goes on to say that "from my own experience, as well as my many years in ministering to others, I have come to realise that we human beings are marvellously adept at building walls; And concealing our true fillings, hiding in dark corners, pretending that we haven't got a problem, and everything is alright with us. We do so because it may seem easier. But avoiding issues will only serve to keep us in bondage and facing them with God's help will set us free" (Meyer, 2015). I also happen to be very good at burying my feelings.

It is so wonderful to be in a relationship with Jesus, because we don't have to hide anything from Him. He already knows everything about us anyway. We can always come to Him and know we will be loved and accepted no matter what we have suffered or how we have reacted to it. Jesus loves us unconditionally. It is empowering, joyous and comforting to know that no matter what I do or say, God loves me anyway.

Once again, Joyce Meyer, put it very aptly. She lived a miserable life, for a long time. Like so many of us, she pretended that everything was fine. We human beings feel we must pretend for the benefit of others, not wanting them to know just how miserable we really feel, and how we lie to ourselves. Sometimes we pretend for so long that we find it hard to separate facts from fiction. Then we don't have courage to face or deal with our difficult issues.

Maybe this describes someone reading this book, or they may know someone with these same problems, like pretending to be one person on the outside and another on the inside. I also pretend to be confident, but in reality, my self-esteem is very low. And what confidence I did have was mostly based on approval from others. My appearance, and accomplishments, and other external factors, were all wrapped up somewhere in between. When the superficial exterior gets stripped away, our most crippling fear is discovered.

CHAPTER III: Life in Jamaica

- *Main characters:*
    - *Bernese*
    - *Hammond (the child abuser)*
    - *Frank (Bernese's boyfriend)*
    - *Mr Long, the stepfather (with the whipping belt)*
    - *Mrs Long, the stepmother (always sick)*
    - *My sister Pauline; (she felt my pain)*

This chapter is about looking back to where it all began. Coming to the realisation that I did not like myself, was a shock to the system, to say the least.

While living in Jamaica, after my mom and aunt had emigrated to England, life took a turn for the worst. I remember, when I was about three years old, I was eating an ice lolly and some of it dripped on the floor that Bernese had just cleaned. Bernese was so upset with me, she complained to her mom, and her mom said: "don't worry she will soon start cleaning it one day". And, oh boy, did she make good her promise! I don't have the exact recollection of everything, because I was so young.

My mom left me as a little girl, but I am not sure at what age my aunt left us. However, I do know that as long as I can remember I suffered abuse at Bernese's hand. When it wasn't her, she would use someone else to dish out my punishment. For example, one day she sent me to the shop to buy something. Not long after, she would send someone to ask for the money back before I could purchase the item she asked me to buy. When I got home the money was gone, and apparently, I was blamed I had spent it on myself. And of course, I was punished for it. As soon as Mr Long came home, she would tell him and he would beat me. No matter how much I would deny it, or try to hide from the beating, he would find me. The belt he used was a man-size belt, which had two sizes to it, one thick and the other thinner. Of course, I would be beaten with the thickest part. Even when I hid under the bed, he would find me. Today, a little girl getting that type of beating would be called child abuse.

I remember us all being invited to Andy's birthday party, the son of our local shop owner and friend. The experience left me with a bitter taste in my mouth. It was while we were seated. Me and my sister could not sit around the table at the same time, so we had to take it in turns. Bernese told me to take the first sitting. Even that she had to spoil for me. When I ate my cake, I was about to get up so that my sister Pauline could have hers. As I was about to get up, Bernese secretly told me to sit back down with force. She told me to eat my sister's slice of the cake. I protested saying the piece was for Pauline. She forced me to eat it. After I ate it, she then proceeded to humiliate me by telling everyone what she said about me was true: that the craven (greedy) girl had eaten all of her sister's cake. I felt mortified and ashamed, as you can guess. Now the whole neighbourhood had me down as a bad girl, a liar and a thief. Because, of that, I have always hated lies and hurting people, even when they hurt me. Because I know what it feels like to be hurt and be falsely accused, I have always treated people the way I want to be treated.

So, instead, I would internalise my pain and sorrow, because it was easier to put the blame on myself than to accuse others. I remember one of the things I had to do to protect myself from being abused in Jamaica: when I was falsely accused, I had to confess to wrongdoing, even though I was innocent. I couldn't take the accusations and prolong beatings any longer, so it was just easier to say 'I did it', or they would not stop the punishment until I confessed. One day we all went out, and when we came home, we saw that our next-door neighbour had tied up her granddaughter and left her in a large rope sack in the back garden, apparently to punish her for her disobedience. All we could hear were her screams, moans and groans. I remember her saying 'Grandma, I promise I won't do it again", over and over again.

Of course, that gave my abusers another idea. They immediately did the same to me. I remember, when the sack was put over my head, I felt so suffocated, and so afraid I couldn't breathe. I thought surely, I was going to die, and to ensure they would stop, I had to confess to something I didn't do.

Moving on, Hammond the rapist would come in the bed that I shared with my sister, pull me away from my sister, who I clung on to for dear life, and sexually abuse me. I went to bed scared every night. I was helpless to stop him from pulling me towards him, and I prayed that my sister would wake up and help me. Although I did not understand what he was doing, I knew it felt wrong. I don't know how long this went on for, nor do I remember my exact age, I was probably about five or six. Eventually, they caught him, or according to them they caught us, and put the blame on me. Can you imagine? I don't know what he told them, but I can guess. This memory is bringing back unwelcomed thoughts to mind, letting me know that the Lord's still working on me. I don't even know why a grown man was allowed to sleep with two children. The only thing I knew then was that he was a solder in the army However, I was recently told that he lived next door, and it would appear that he was the cousin of the people I was staying with. Pauline did not suffer from abuse in the same way that I did, but I know she had her own fair share of bad memories, so I won't speak for her. I believe that she was more protected because Mr Long, Bernese's birth father, was also her birth father (un-related to me). We both suffered hunger, we hardly had much food to eat. I realise that there was no sense in going to Mrs Long, for help, because Mrs Long would just support her daughter, because she was a very sickly woman. I don't remember her doing me any real harm, and she died early.

My other abuser (non-sexual, in this case) was Bernese's boyfriend, who would routinely throw things aimed at my head whenever he visited with Bernese, with her permission. Between them they would both gang up on me violently; if God wasn't protecting me, I would have had some brain damage by now. I am not sure now how I ended up becoming an academic, but God, I do believe however that was the beginning of me suffering with depression. I remember the Long's organised kindergarten home-schooling in their back yard. I was very rarely allowed to attend since I would be doing constant housework. But I do remember us briefly attending mainstream school. One highlight of my life was when I first looked at the illustrated children's Bible, and I fell in love with Jesus. My education really began from then and when I came to England.

I remember my sister and I got very little food to eat. Many nights we went to bed hungry, and along with that, Bernese would always accuse me of stealing her dad's food, and money. I remember on my birthday mom would send us clothes, shoes, and other goods, which went to other people, and even my birthday cake that mom sent, if it hadn't got rotten on the boat, I wouldn't have got any. I had a couple of friends living across the road who believed in me. They were a God send. I remember when mom heard what was happening to me, and decided to bring me to England, I told my two friends, and one said, "I know what you should do. When Bernese takes you to the Airport, you should take a knife and stab her in her back, and leave". Bless her.

I remember, when Bernese realised I was going to England, she pulled me aside talking nice to me for the first time. She was checking if I was going to tell mum what she did to me. What else could I say? "But no, sister Bernese". However, as soon as mom asked, I told her the truth, and of course she wrote to them, and they denied it. I thank mom for believing in me. After that, I did not talk much about what I went through. I just wanted to forget about it. But I realised that it wasn't going to forget me and it did much damage to my system. When I came to know the Lord, He made me realise that I needed healing from past hurts and that my pain, long buried, was holding me back from living a whole, healthy life. This reminds me of the woman with the issue of blood; for 12 years she suffered, and she was healed just by touching the hem of Jesus's garment. Her story is told in Mark 5:25-34. I realised that I could also be healed, by believing, reaching out, and acting in faith.

CHAPTER IV: Emigration to England, met Mom

I remember how cold London was. I had my first experience of winter snow. I remember feeling very cold in my little frilly dress, the ones we would wear in Jamaica for special occasions. I was not dressed for winter, but thoughts of seeing my mum kept me warm. I was so excited to see her that the cold did not matter. That moment I laid my eyes on her; it was like all the bad things that I had been through had been forgotten. But to my dismay, mom didn't recognise me. "That's not my Angela", mom exclaimed, shocked. She had to look at my name tag to check if I was really her daughter when she realised that I was actually her. She was disappointed. She asked what they had done to me. I remember embarking on the long journey home from the airport; everything was a blur, as it was on the plane. I had knots in my stomach, I remember confusing thoughts going round in my mind, repeatedly. I was not familiar with English weather or English food so I thought I was probably going to freeze to death or die of starvation. Then I really started to feel the cold, and couldn't feel my fingers or toes. I tried to cover up my hurt and disappointment, with complaints about the cold weather. However, meeting my British brothers and sisters was such a happy occasion for me. It helped take my mind off things. There were four of them. The two older ones were reserved, but when I went and held out my hands to the two younger ones, they were so responsive. I fell in love with them. Then mom had her youngest boy later on, when we were more grown.

Good times spent with Mom

One of my best times spent alone with Mom was watching her favourite movies: cowboy movies, and old Hollywood glam, action and mystery. Basically, escapism They became my favourites too, even to this date. These were the times that I felt closer to mom. We would sit and talk about all the stars from old films. Another happy time spent with Mom was when we would go shopping together, and sit down to eat a hot dog together, and just generally have some alone time. But I also enjoyed some of the times spent with my siblings. Mom would teach us her old childhood games that she learned as a youth in Jamaica, such as nursery rhymes, old folk's tales, riddles, and ghost stories, and she would act them out with us in plays. We would have singing and dancing competitions. Sometimes dad would be present, and we would all try to outdo each other to impress them. These times were enjoyable for all.

Time spent with other relatives

- *Main characters:*
  - ○ *Auntie Olive*
  - ○ *Uncle Johnny*
  - ○ *Cousin Molly*
  - ○ *Cousin Nathan*

Times with Auntie Olive were hilarious, and eventful. My Aunty Olive was such a character; she just loved Wrestling and Boxing. She would visit us every Saturday, during Saturday Sports, and when she visited, there would be uproar in the house. She would be away with every punch, and it would be as if she was really at the ringside with her favourite wrestler/boxer. Shouting at the top of her voice, "kill him, kill him", "get him, slaughter him", "jump on him, go on, get him". And she would be making hand gestures, twirling, and turning her body in sync with the wrestler, or rolling with the punches with the boxer. You would think that she was in the ring. When she would fall off the chair with legs dangling in the air, we would help her get back up, but she would just continue with her antics. Everyone would be caught up with her enthusiasm. We were roaring with laughter; she was so infectious. How I used to look forward to her visits! They were the good old days. I missed Auntie Olive very much, after she passed away.

Uncle Johnny was also the life and soul of the party, and even to this day he is still doing his party piece, whether a funeral, wedding, or any other family social gathering. If he wasn't there, he would be sorely missed. Firstly, he would give his speech, whether you wanted him to or not, and take his own time. Then he would dance with a glass of whatever spirit he was drinking on top of his head, and he would do this without spilling a drop. Then there was the limbo, where he would get way down low, and we would have to help him get up again. I used to wander how his back never gave up. These days, even in his old age, he is still at parties, giving speeches and singing, although not a singer in any shape or form, but we love him dearly, because he doesn't care what anyone thinks, and we know that whatever he does, he does it from the heart, and we love him. Like Auntie Olive, we also looked forward to his visit, and he would never visit us without bringing treats and gifts, ranging from Kentucky fried chicken, fish and chips, and different types of sweets and crisps. God bless you, Uncle Johnny!

Then there were their children, our cousin Molly and Nathan. We used to have so much fun when they came around. Nathan was always the intellectual one. He would always be studying and never have time for fun. I believe that Nathan encouraged me to go into further education.

Oh, but we would always get into mischief. We would always find something comical in every situation. We would look at everyone and point out their flaws, and then erupt into fits of giggling, and laughter. Then get told off for making so much noise. When Molly came to spend time with us over the holidays, we could never stop laughing. Molly was like her dad, uncle Johnny. She was very entertaining. Molly was fair in complexion and had long thick dark. Curly hair. There was always drama about washing her hair. She would scream, and scream, and scream, and then scream again you would think she was being murdered, but mom would continue holding her down, saying she was going to wash "this mop" if it is the last thing she did. And as she got older, and became an even naughtier teenager, she would tell us stories of her escapades. How, when Uncle Johnny went to sleep thinking that she had gone to bed, she would climb out of the window and go to a party, without him knowing. I remember thinking I could do the same. And I did contemplate it, but we lived on the second floor, which was too high for me. Not only that, I was too afraid of mom. It was like she could see right through me, and she would found out, and I would get a beating for my trouble. I didn't like the type of beating mom would give me. Although she beat my other siblings, she was more careful with them. When my other siblings were being beaten, they would always hold the belt, for each other, to stop mom. But when she was beating me, they would just laugh and say, "you cry funny". I just felt like she was taking her anger out on me because she did not like me very much. She used to say, "I hate your ways", and I would end up with either a black eye or a swollen lip. I remember going to school in the aftermath of the latter, and as soon as my school friends saw me, they knew exactly what had gone down. No matter how much I denied it, they proceeded to tease me throughout the day, making me feel worse. But that's children for you.

CHAPTER V: Life at Home with my Family

- *Main Characters:*
  - *Me, Angela*
  - *Mom Maria*
  - *Dad James*
  - *Brothers and sisters*
    - *Paul*
    - *Mervin*
    - *Daniella*
    - *Duncan the baby*
    - *Edna*

I was always trying some form or other to get mom to notice me more. Life at home had its ups and downs. I ran away from home several times, because I felt unloved and unappreciated. I tried everything to get my mom's attention. I just wanted her to show me love the way I believed that she should show it. Little did I realise that she went through her own childhood trauma, one that kept her emotionally unavailable. But how can you show love if you never experienced it yourself?

I remember once I wanted to stay up late with her, after everyone had gone to bed, and watch her favourite TV program. I was dreading when she would tell me to go to bed, because that was one of the only times I felt close to her, after the others had gone to sleep. When she did utter those words, I was so unhappy and I did not want to leave her side. One time, I went upstairs, I found my school's compass, and proceeded to force it into the skin of my hands until it bled and tore, just to get her attention. Then I went back down stairs to show her the state of my hands, believing she would give me sympathy. It had the opposite effect: she looked at me angrily, and said, "You stupid girl, go to your bed!". So, of course, I went to bed in tears feeling rejected. When you have been away from your mother for so long, and full of hurt, you want to make up for lost time. You feel that only your mother can heal your brokenness.

Over the years I always tried one thing or another to get my mom's attention. I just wanted her to say "I love you, Angie". When she was upset with me, she would call me Angela. So, because of that, I went through a period where I did not like my name, and I even changed it once by deed poll. Because Mom found it hard to show love to her children, I don't remember my mom ever hugging me. Even when I hugged her. Yet, she showed her love through food. Being in a family of seven, you had to fight for attention, my stepdad included. He just seemed starved of mom's affection.

I remember my friends saying to me stop torturing myself trying to get my mother to love me. "You will make yourself ill", they'd say, but it was hard to listen to them. As I mentioned earlier, it is hard to give what you haven't been given.

Later on, I realised that one of the reasons mom sent for me was so that I would fit in in with my British siblings, because when she left me I was very fair in complexion. The way she reacted when she picked me up at the airport is still lodged in my memory. I remember how shocked she was to see the change in me, and how she almost refused to accept me as her child. I don't think she ever got over it. Anyone who really knew mom, knew that she preferred fair complexion to dark. We know that is a slave's mentality. I am not saying that she did not love me. After all, I am her first fruit, and she stayed with me until I was age three. I understood mom didn't like herself much either. To make me more presentable, she would send me to Mrs D, the local hairdresser, who used a hot iron comb from a gas stove to straighten out my hair. I remember getting burned a lot. When that did not work to mom's satisfaction, she bought me my first wig. I must admit I was proud of my wig. Everyone commented on it favourably; it also made me look older. That was not a good thing though, all it did was encourage the daddy figures, who should know better. I guess that is what started my love of wigs.

Mom did not believe me

One bone of contention I had with mom was that she didn't believe me, when I told her that my stepdad was acting inappropriately towards me when we were alone. He would touch me, and kiss me, especially after telling me off for something that I had done wrong. That was apparently my reward. I made excuses for him because I looked like mum, and mum did not give him enough attention. When I told her, my mum called me a liar and accused me of wanting to send my stepdad to prison, which was far from the truth. I just wanted her to believe me, tell him to stop. It was that simple.

Also, at that time, a lot of men old enough to be my father, or grandfather, would be always be hitting on me, telling me that I was ripe for the picking, and because I was young and shy, they thought they could get away with it. When I told Mom immediately, she believed me, and would ask why I didn't tell her before. I asked why it mattered to her; she did not believe me when I told her about dad. She went silent, for a moment, as if she had not heard me. She then asked me to name those men who would make such remarks, so that she would deal with them, and she did.

When I look back now, I think mom must have given me some love, being her first child. I lived from birth to age 3 with her, and I didn't have to share her then, and I believe that between her and Auntie Florie, I was given love. Auntie Florie always showed me love, and I believe that; it was that love that helped me carry on through all the pain, heartache, and suffering that I was going through at the hands of strangers.

Believe me, I am not writing this book to hurt anyone. This is not the case, and it is not the first time that I have spoken about my past. Nor am I doing it for the glory, because the glory belongs to the Lord, who instructed me to write my story, and I must tell my truth to get my healing. If you are not revealing, how can you get your healing?

I even amazed myself that even through all of it, I was able to love my brothers and sisters unconditionally, and then later on, my son and my husband. So even during self-dislike, resentment, and rejection, I am amazed that I could give love to anyone, but I believe that the Lord has me covered, every step of the way.

Going back to my stepdad, despite everything, he treated me well. I remember him beating me once, and saying he would never beat me again. He would leave the beating to mom, and he kept his promise. He could hardly tell me off. So, I had to separate what he did to me from how he treated me. I remember when he died, I was so grief-stricken. I cried practically the whole day, I don't know why, and to this day I still don't know why. All I can think of is that I must have cared for him much more than I thought. I did not cry at my mom's passing nearly as much as I did when my stepdad died, even though I loved her dearly.

As previously stated, during those years, I would run away from home, times and again, and come back for one reason or another. Each time I would go back home because of necessity, or because I missed my family, but then I would soon leave again until, one day, I just stop coming back. Sometimes I would not see my family, for three to five years. Mom kept saying the door was always open, but within that open door, I did not feel wanted, and the cross of ten was on the wall, as we say in Jamaica,, meaning that I was going to fear badly out there, so I had something to prove, and so I did. Thank you, lord.

CHAPTER VI: I realised I loved my family unconditionally

The realisation that I loved my family unconditionally, in spite of everything, was always a wake-up call. Then, when I finally went back home after I had grown up, I remember bravely knocking on the door; mom would open the door, and look at me with anger, and leave me outside, closing the door again, only for me to knock again. I stood and waited, and it was dad who welcomed me in, calling me the prodigal daughter, although I don't remember having any riches to squander.

Another memory I have of home life was when one day I was taking a family photo. Mom told me that I spoiled the picture; she would always talk negatively about my dark complexion. I used to wonder if she knew she also has a dark complexion. I remember feeling very rejected, wishing that I had a fair complexion, like the rest of my siblings, so that I could fit in better. One day I even started to bleach my skin. I began by just wanting to clear up the dark patches around my face and neck. I started to like the colour I was seeing, so I spread to whole parts of my body. I don't think I fully realised what I was doing, because it was not that I didn't like my complexion; I think I did because, in secondary school, I was always around dark complexion girls who were very proud of their dark skin. I know God is in this revelation. I just wanted to fit in better with the family, so that I would get more attention from mom. The first time I realised that the change was visible, was when I visited one of my friends. She noticed but did not mention it. She had another visiting friend who looked at my son, whose complexion was a little light, and told him he looked as fair as me. I think I felt good to hear that because I was fed up with people looking at my son and thinking that he was my sister's child. It wasn't until my brother Marvin told me to stop bleaching my skin. Then I had another wake-up call, and realised what I was doing. I immediately stopped.

Jesus wants us to receive his love. Just know that when you feel unloved and rejected, He cares about everything that concerns us. For some of us, it is hard to believe, especially when we are either fatherless, motherless, or both. And when we think of the bad things that we have done in our lifetime, we need to know that Jesus will forgive us, and when we ask Him to, we need to accept that He has forgiven us. He loves us unconditionally. We must take it to heart, so that when we suffer the rejection in one form or another, we do not blame God for our predicament, because of our unbelief. Know that only love can conquer hate. As the song goes, "Jesus loves me, this I know, for the Bible tells me so. Little ones to Him belong; they are weak, but He is strong". In addition, Jesus is the lover of your soul, and you matter a great deal to God. You are special and precious in His sight. The Bible says, "when my father and my mother forsake me, the Lord will take me up" (Psalms 27:10). God wants us to live in peace and good health. In other words, He wants us to enjoy life every day. Jesus said, "My peace I leave with you; my peace I give to you. Not as the world gives do I give to you…" (John 14:27). Even though we have troubles and face disturbing issues, we can still experience the peace that Jesus offers because it surpasses all human understanding. Therefore, we can still feel peace in our hearts even when everything seems to be falling apart in our lives.

I remember when my mom couldn't deal with my issues anymore. She would say, "I wish you would become a Christian and change", but she really meant, "Shut your mouth, sweep everything under the proverbial carpet, so that I don't have to deal with it anymore". I remember resenting her for saying it; and I thought, "As if God could change anything." However, some years later, she got her wish. And now I know that was the best thing she could have ever wished for me. When I found God, I remember wishing I had acknowledged Him earlier in my life. I know I could have spared myself from much heartache, if I had only called on His name earlier. Accepting Jesus as my Lord and Saviour marked the beginning of a long and difficult road to recovery, but I don't regret it for one minute. It was the making of me. You see, when you keep your pain hidden, the devil uses it against you, and if you are not careful, you can turn into an unforgiving, bitter, twisted, and angry person, especially angry at God, the world, and sometimes even yourself. As mentioned before, how can you receive healing if you're not revealing? So, let go and let God in. We inflict upon ourselves a great deal of pain and sorrow by burying our hurts deep within, locking them away in a vault. Sometimes, we go as far as holding a metaphorical funeral and inviting others to join in mourning. We then clutch their sympathies like a security blanket, using them as a shield to prevent further hurt. Only a unique combination key can unlock this vault. The truth is, we often resist letting go and prevent others from coming close enough to assist us. Here's the important part: God holds the key to your combination lock, waiting for you to reach out and ask for help to unlock the door of your self-imposed vault.

It's as if we're trapped in a time capsule. Similar to the movie, Frozen, we isolate ourselves in an ice castle, guarded by a pit-bull at the door warning others to proceed with caution. This behaviour confines our emotions, leading to self-imprisonment. Unfortunately, this isn't good, as it can lead to depression, and anger turned inward, along with anxiety and other mental health issues.

Without allowing Jesus in, healing and transformation can't take place. Similarly, depression can manifest in various ways, like consuming excessive sugar and salt, experiencing sleep deprivation, and even oversleeping can contribute to it. This may also lead to weight problems and their associated challenges. Additionally, being surrounded by negative influences can steal your joy, as they seek to share their unhappiness, alongside yours. This won't be the last time I enthuse this point.

People might perceive you as problem-free due to your happiness, yet you're aware of your challenges. However, you don't wear them on your sleeve; you trust God to guide you through. We all face challenges, and our response to them determines our path. "The Word encourages us to have hope in God, for we will praise Him yet" (Psalm 42:11).

To aid an unhappy individual, don't lower yourself; instead, encourage them to rise to your level. Maintain your happiness, safeguard your joy. God intends for us to dwell in calm delight, regardless of circumstances. It's essential to opt for sustained happiness; prioritize joy in your life, regardless of external factors.

CHAPTER VII: Starting primary school

Because my education in Jamaica was limited, starting school in England felt unfamiliar. I recall feeling quite behind, unsure how I could manage to catch up, but I had a strong willingness to learn. However, I sensed the teachers weren't putting in enough effort with me and other Caribbean girls. We struggled to see ourselves in the English curriculum, as Caribbean teaching primarily focused on rote learning, which involved repetition. Our materials featured characters like Bob and Nola, who were black. In contrast, in England, it was Peter and Jane, who were white. Consequently, I channelled most of my energy into playing and drawing, activities I enjoyed. Schoolwork posed a significant challenge, and homework was even tougher, but my mom did her best to assist me. True learning began when I entered secondary school and lived with my aunt in Wellingborough. The teachers put in a real effort with me there, and from then on, I started to engage with my lessons.

Then, I delved into reading and taught myself how to read. I discovered that I not only enjoyed it but loved it. This led me to start with reading comics, then progress to romance novels. I later ventured into English literature, including plays. Role play became a passion, and I'd even teach my sisters how to act and join in the fun. I'd sketch out characters and add colour to them, even paint them.

I also liked sports, especially the 100-meter relay, and a game similar to baseball known as 'rounders'. At school, the young me would play a mean game of Jacks, and this continued even at home after school. I distinctly remember the elation on my face after winning a game; it was a feeling of triumph. Consequently; I became the one to beat. I had to have something of my own, didn't I?

From my primary school, I remember black boys were scared, resulting in 3 girls who found themselves sharing 1 boyfriend, the most popular one of course, and I was among them. No matter how much the other boys would crave for my attention, I wasn't interested. Instead of having a boyfriend of my own, I was happy to share the most popular one with other girls, which came with conditions. We girls were jealous, because everyone wanted to be his number one, and because of that we would sometimes fight it out. I remember being told by one of the girl, that she was going to fight me after school, so I got scared, because I knew that there was going to be more than one girl I had to contend with. So, I proceeded to hide and wait until everyone had gone home. When I came out of my hiding place, only to be met with more than three girls vying for my blood, I realised that I did not outsmart them, they outsmarted me. I thought with resignation I had to take my beating, and lump it.

One day I remember coming home telling my siblings all about my boyfriend, and how he kissed me (only on the cheeks of course). This was just innocent banter that just made me feel better about myself. Although I told them not to tell mom, they would blackmail me for treats, and to stop them, I had to bribe them by giving them sweets. And of course, when the sweets ran out, they would tell mom, and I certainly got it from her. But I was certainly not short of admirers, even though I thought I was not good looking enough. Coming from a family, where fair is good looking, and dark is not so much, it was hard to think different.

However, as I got older, there was this one boyfriend, who was older, that used to call me his 'pretty little thing'. How I loved to hear those words, because those endearing words were my lifeline, because I craved affection. When I did not have lunch money, he would give me some of his lunch and he generally took care of me. He helped give me the confidence in my own beauty; he would always boost my self-confidence. "The Lord, gives us beauty for ashes…" (Isaiah 61:3). You realise if you see yourself ugly, some people will see it too, and use it against you; it's like spirit recognise spirit. No matter how my friends would tell me how pretty I was, I did not believe it. Some people would use your insecurity against you, to help them deal with their own insecurity. Two things I did not like in myself, my up and down weight, and not being pretty enough.

CHAPTER VIII: Life in secondary school

I went to secondary school in Wellingborough, Northamptonshire, when living with my aunt Florie. I had very good teaching there.

Although I did enjoy my schooling, it was sometimes too quiet compared to school in London. In Wellingborough the teachers were so patient with me, and there were a lot of them to go around, so I learnt a lot. I had more opportunities to learn and do more sports. I remember learning how to play hockey, and I loved it; I had a healthy rounded education. Even math was easier to understand, even though it was not a subject that I shone in. Give me English, History, Art and Cookery, and I would ace it; I really had a healthy rounded education.

I remember having disagreement with a girl called Jemma, but we argued it out. Then another friend also had a disagreement with Jemma. Instead of letting them sort it out among themselves, we all waded in and got into a physical fight with her. Everyone began to hit her, including me. There were so many of us hitting poor Jemma, I don't even think she knew where the blows were coming from. That wasn't my finest hour. From then on, I decided that, in future, if two of my friends had a disagreement, I would leave them to sort it out with each other, and not take sides, unless it is to act as a peacemaker.

Secondary school in London was more overcrowded, and teachers had very little time for one-on-one interactions. Because I missed my brothers and sisters, I preferred to stay in London. Even though I had everything for my comfort, sometimes living with Aunt Florie made me feel lonely away from mom. So, I kept going back and forth between schools. In London, I attended an all-girl's secondary school that was majority black girls. The teachers gave more preferential treatment to the gifted children, which meant that they didn't, have much time to devote to those who needed more attention.

I remember my Maths teacher, who was an Indian man and sometimes taught us and sometimes didn't; I suppose it depended on what mood he was in that day. Since we were in the lowest class, it didn't matter much to him.

However, as previously stated, I excelled in the subjects I loved. However, it is funny how one can get out of one's craft if one stops practicing.

Secondary school in London was very cliquey and consisted of the following groups:

Top Girls or the group I was not allowed in:

- Marvia, who was number one.
- Diana, the admirer
- The Big Mouth, Aubrey's admirer.
- Ruby the Admirer
- Alfia, the admirer
- Yalia, the admirer.

My group was the outsiders, of which I was the leader:

- Me
- Aniya
- Paula
- Yannis

Our school had a bad reputation for fighting. Some of the girls would go around to other schools and pick a fight. Of course I rarely went with them; I always had better ways to occupy my time. I remember there were twins named the 'Banton Twins', always getting into fight, and not always of their own making, simply because they were so thin. The other girls were always quick pick to fights with them, because they looked like a gush of wind would blow them down, and so they would always get challenged. The Banton Twins were lovely girls and knew how to defend themselves.

Some of the girls were a little rough around the edges, and very aggressive. They would form in groups, and the most popular girl would be at the head, and if you dared to cross them you would know about it. Any other group would not matter. I remember that in my first year at school, one member of the group, who had a big mouth, would hand books to her friends nicely when the teacher told her to give out books for the day's lesson. However, my friend and I would have books thrown at us so hard that we had to duck to avoid it from hitting us in the head. Once, I decided to challenge her. I remember asking her if she thought we were pigs. I used the word 'Hogg', in Jamaican dialect. That did not go down well. She looked at me with such a penetrating look, as if her looks could kill. I knew that I would be in for it after class; in fact, she came over to me, along with her group members, and slapped me in the face. It brought tears to my eyes. I protested, but was helpless to do anything about it for fear of reprisal from her clique gang. Similarly, the same thing happened to me with another girl. Everyone called her by her pet name 'Rudy'. When I decided to also call her Rudy, she gave me the biggest slap across my face. I was sure everyone could see her hand print on my face. I asked myself what was up with these girls and their bullying ways. Once again I could not do anything, because of her clique gang.

After that I just decided to bide my time, and my time did come, as my popularity developed, and hers dwindled down. She became someone that nobody wanted to be around, because she had hygiene issues. She smelled so bad that no one wanted to give her the time of day. Sometimes I thank God, that He had a hand in my life! But I felt so bad for her, that I became her friend. I even visited her home, and could see that she had been neglected. We weren't that old; we were probably between the ages of twelve and thirteen.

I have always been the champion of the underdogs, for want of a better world. When the older girls would have fights with the younger ones, I would always intervene, letting the older girls know that they should know better, and that they should be setting better role models for the young girls. Another girl began to apparently spread untrue rumours about me. And because my popularity was growing, I was required to act, and show my mettle, so both her and my group came face to face. Each one of us stood in front of each other, and I stood tall with arms akimbo, looking at her in the eye, saying. "Yes, miss Carol, I heard that you have been spreading rumours about me, and that you are going to fight me. What do you have to say for yourself?" Of course, she denied it the moment I advanced towards her, ready to give her a blow. She bent her head down, with both arms on her head, to avoid the blow, begging me not to hit her. Then I realized that she was scared of me, so I just said; "You are not worth my trouble".

From then on, I was in the popular group. So, not only did I have more friends in my year group. I also had friends among the older girls who were the year above me. The older girls would always protect me, and I would protect the younger girls. Prior to that I remembered when anyone wanted to fight me, I would cry at the thought of the fight, but the girls thought that it was because I was scared, so they called me a cry-baby. They did not realise, however, that was the time I was at my most dangerous. It's a bit like Kandi in "The Real Housewives of Atlanta": she always cries before she fights.

Looking back at another time, one day a group of us went to cookery class at another school, and after our class was over, I was attacked by a group of boys, who tried to rape me, and what was worse was that one of my school friends, Yvonne, just looked on and did not do much to help me. I remember being petrified. I called her for help, and she just laughed with the boys. I screamed so loud, and fought so hard, that I did not know my own strength. I think they got scared, as they saw someone coming, so they let me go. There was also another time when I had left home and was just relying on friends or relatives to take me in. Once I stayed at a school friend's home, and she put me in her spare room to stay. While there, an older boy also tried to rape me, and once again I had to fight him off, so

I had to leave once again. I went to stay with an auntie who lived very close to my school, but she told me that she had to let my mom know where I was. I protested, but to no avail. The message that mom gave my auntie was 'the door is always open'. This memory just came up, from beyond the grave. I had forgotten about it. As the Lord brought it to mine, I had to forgive her.

Another time there was this fair-skinned girl in the year below me. She took an instant dislike to me. I can't remember why, so we kept out of each other's way, until one day, I was out shopping with mom, in Brixton, and we bumped in to each other. As we were about to do our usual avoiding-each-other thing, I heard Mom say "Hallo Sharleen, how are you?", and then proceeded to have a conversation. "How is your Mom? And the family?...". My heart sank, then with a smile mom added, "Angela, meet your cousin Sharleen". We were both stunned. Surely she cannot be my cousin, I thought. Sharleen and mom continued to talk for a while, so I reluctantly joined in, for conversation's sake. Because we did not like each other at school, we both pinned on a false smile. Then it was time for us to say goodbye to each other, and mom proceeded to explain how we were related, through this cousin and that cousin, and so on. Back at school, we decided to put our differences aside, and became cousin-friends. We both must have decided this over the weekend, because from then on, we always stuck up for each other. She was so proud to tell everyone that we were cousins. From then on, we always greeted each other with "Hi cuz!".

One day, as I was walking to one of my classes, I saw my cousin in great distress, running towards me, completely petrified. She was asking for my help. In quick succession, I saw the girl that I previously had contention with, running after her with a knife taken from her cookery class. Looking back now, I wonder if she had some mental health issues. I stopped my cousin in her tracks, and told her not to run from her because she was a coward. "If she sees you running," I said, "she will continue to run after you". However, my cousin did not stop to listen, and continued to run. So, I ran after them to try to put a stop to it. Before I could do anything, they ran straight into a teacher, and ended up in detention.

CHAPTER IX: The early days after leaving home and my after-school's club with Lorna

I left home between the age of fourteen and fifteen. I remember it well. The school had an after-school's club, so I asked mom if I could go. She refused to allow me. I just couldn't understand her objections, since my siblings were allowed to go to any school activity or social occasion they wanted to attend. She rarely allowed me to go on any school outing or function when all my friends could go, and they would tease me so. The one time she allowed me to go to one of my friend's birthday parties, just as the party was on the way, I had to go home, because she got it in her head, that I would get up to no good.

There were no valid reasons behind it, and she gave me no freedom. The last straw came after she refused to let me go to the after-school club, especially when the teacher would bring us all home after in her mini-bus. So, I decided to go anyway. Mom wasn't happy with that, but I needed that outlet for my sanity. When the teacher brought me home and knocked on the door, mom wouldn't let me in. After ringing the bell continuously, my teacher gave up and found a place for me to stay. That's when I first left home, and I went straight into foster care. After that, I stayed with Lorna's friends for a while. Eventually, I got into a hostel, and I did not visit home for several years.

I enjoyed my after-school club very much. We would play games, listen to music, go to visit museums, attend theatre plays. Through this, I developed a love for drama/acting/singing. Even after I left home, I still went to the club. We would meet up for dinner, go for long country walks, and go on youth trips. One of the things I remember is when we took a trip to Suffolk, one of England's most beautiful and scenic countryside areas. We had so much fun there, all girls together.

I remember two sisters, Dora and Nora. They were real characters. They always wore tight trousers, and after every meal, no matter how stuffed they were, they would suffer the discomfort because they would never undo their trousers. According to them, if they did, the stomach would expand, and they would put on weight. We all tried to copy them, but we couldn't stand the tightness. They were such a delight and a laugh.

I remember learning to ride a bicycle when I was about fifteen. One day, I decided to go out on my own, to get some practice. I got on the bicycle, but I had no idea how to get off. So, I began careering down the country lane. It was hilly and I picked up the pace, while rolling down the hill. Although the road was quiet, my pace got faster and faster, and the bicycle was out of my control. I decided to slam on the brakes, and this action immediately threw me flying over the front of the bike, headfirst, into an open field that broke my fall. I was so lucky. I thank God I landed well; my Angel must have had me in his hands. I was slightly bruised and sore, but no broken bones. I was glad that no one saw me, that would have been too embarrassing. However, when the girls saw how I was limping, I foolishly told them what happened. Of course they roared with laughter. Those were some of the happy times of my life.

At the time, I remember that when I visited my family neighbourhood, I would only visit friends and neighbours who lived in the vicinity, close to home, but never visiting home. And of course, if they asked me what the problem was, I would tell them, but it would eventually get back to my family, and they would deny it. It wasn't helping my cause, anyway, so I soon realised it would be better if I just kept my mouth shut. My motto was always this: the truth will always come out in the end anyway. And it did.

CHAPTER X: Then There was sibling rivalry

It wasn't until after I left home and entered my twenties that I began to have a better relationship with my mom. It started off rocky, but I understood her a little better. It took mom a while to forgive me, because she was still angry with me for leaving home. At first, I would visit after work, but dad was the only one who welcomed me. Mom took her time, but she eventually warmed up to me. Once she saw that I had no animosity towards her, she began to open her heart more towards me. Since then, before every visit home, I would call ahead and ask mom to prepare my favourite Caribbean food and she would prepare it, topped off with rum and raisin ice cream. Mom would make sure it was there when I visited, and if it wasn't, she would send one of my siblings to buy it.

This went on for a while, until one day, mom stopped preparing anything for me. I didn't know why, but I guess that maybe my siblings did not like me receiving mom's special attention. I kind of felt like a Joseph, the black sheep of the family. However, I may have bragged to my siblings that mom was giving me preferential treatment, so partly my fault. I knew it wasn't going to sit well. I think that they may have complained to mom. Up to then, I used to enjoy my visits home, but when our relationship changed again, I went back to feeling unloved because mom showed her love through food.

It took years later for me to realise that she did love me, but she did not know how or was afraid to show it. And also, in those days the older sibling did every household chore. I remembered that after each meal everybody would leave the table and go relax in the front room, and have fun, leaving me all alone in the dining room to clear and wash everything up and more. I used to feel so left out, I would sing this Elvis Priestley's 1970 song, 'The Wonder of You'. It says, "When no one else can understand me, when everything I do is wrong, you give me hope and consolation you give me strength to carry on...". I sometimes felt like I was a slave to my younger siblings. But the one thing I did admire my stepdad for was that, every Saturday, to be fair to me, he would make all my brothers and sisters clean the house from top to bottom, at the same time. It was like our chore's day. Mom, on the other hand, did not ask my siblings to do any chores. I think she did not like housework very much, and one thing I knew was that dad did not force mom to do much. If he wanted food, he would just cook it, and take off the pressure from mom. My dad wasn't the easiest person to live with, but he loved mom. It was during this time that I ran away from home several times, first at age thirteen and I went to a children's home, but mom refused to pay, so I had to return home. Another time I was sent to a foster home temporarily. When it was time to leave, I asked my foster parents if I could stay with them permanently, but it was not possible, so once again I had to return again, and eventually left home age fourteen.

Chapter XI: I left school in 1973 and almost immediately I started my first job

I started my first job at the age of sixteen. I worked in local government, and I began in the post room as a clerk. I then worked my way up to executive officer, then to chief executive, and borough solicitor. This continued my education in life. My command of the English language was fully developed, through my work with the Borough's top solicitors, with whom I was attending Court sessions. I would give evidence in the borough's cases between landlords and tenants, and among other things.

During my time working for the borough of Southwark, I was given the opportunity to develop and express my creative side, and get recognition from my peers. Along the way, I met some good friends, and had some good role models to aspire to. I had a good support network. After a while I realised that I needed to further educate myself, because I saw people who had started work after me getting promoted. Not thinking highly of me, even the fragile status that I had acquired in my workplace had dwindled along with my confidence, which became non-existent, and my self-esteem, which hit an all-time low. I felt stuck in a rut both in my career, and in my private life. I longed for the days when I was thought highly of and was invited to almost every after-work function.

When I performed at the theatre, all my work colleagues and friends came to support me. My boss would also allow me to hang in the office the paintings that I drew; I genuinely knew they liked me and my paintings. This pattern of existence went on for a while but then I found myself in a rut. I guess all good things must come to an end sometimes. Maybe, if things had stayed the same, I probably would have stayed there until I retired, but then I would not have done my degree, so I must be thankful for the change.

Sean, my unexpected, delightful gift from God

I became unexpectedly pregnant with Sean at the age of 27. During my pregnancy with Sean, I decided to move on to higher education, while still working part time with the Southwark Council. I wanted to educate myself and help my son at the same time. I did not want to be ignorant of the school's system, and I did not want Sean to struggle the way I did. So I started a course of self-improvement, to try to answer some of the questions that I had no answers for, and I enrolled myself into higher education. I began by doing an 'A-Level access to Higher Education' course, which propelled me into the Polytechnic, then on to university which led me to passing my first degree. I acquired a Bachelor of Art's Degree, which I passed with Honours. I then went on to do a Master in Caribbean Culture and History. This peaked my desire to know more about my Caribbean heritage and culture. As I took to motherhood, my son became my pride and joy. I was so happy to know that finally, I had a child of my own, to pour all that love that I had inside of me. Sean added much joy and pleasure to my life. God gave me a very loving and caring son, who gave me unconditional love. God used Sean to help bring out the best in me, and I realise that I wanted the best for my son. I decided to educate him to the max, and in fact, I started educating Sean from he was in my belly, using a well-known American technique called 'hothousing' where you start educating the child from the womb, by reading intellectual type literature to the unborn foetus. With hothousing, he had a better start than I did. Before Sean could walk, he could read and recognise words, and not long after he could write his name. From there, he was then in the top set in his class. It was a pleasure to hear him read. He had and still has a very commanding tone to his voice. He had a stint in private school, which helped to further his academic ability. He developed a love for football, and wanted to go pro. But as well as supporting him and his love for the game, I encouraged him to pursue higher education, as backup plan, in case he didn't get scouted. He agreed to it, he went on to successfully complete a Bachelor of Arts degree in Business and Commerce, which has served him well in his business acumen today.

When it came to me, I was still searching for the meaning of life. I found that even after gaining qualifications, there were even more questions. I was still empty, and searching. I have always been artistic and multitalented. Because of this, it was difficult to know which way to go. I love to cook, I bake, I draw, I can sing and dance, and also act. I even had some opera training, which I should have advanced in, but didn't. I acted and sang in in my first musical at the Young Vic Theatre, based on the Depression Era and called 'They Shoot Horses Don't They?'. I had the raw talent but did not home in on them. I continued, until one day I was chosen by the BBC to feature in their education programme, about my life as one of the first, matured student to go to university. They made a brief film about my life. The BBC filmed me with my son at play, when he was about three and a half. The BBC also filmed me at my university, the Polytechnic, and at Southwark Council where I worked at the time. This led to my first live interview at the BBC Studios.

After that, I had big ambitions. I dreamed about becoming the English Oprah Winfrey, especially after the BBC said that I had a face and a presence, for the camera. But because I wanted to pursue my master's degree, I did not get in touch with my BBC contact until a year later, when the number I had was changed. That was one of my biggest regrets, with having no-one who believed enough in me to push me towards achieving my goal. It remained a dream I just wished I had followed through.

CHAPTER XII: My self-esteem was at an all-time low

Over the years I would start something but wouldn't finish it, never quite sure how to go about doing what I wanted to do. I had a fear of failure, and I ended up doing more courses on self-improvement, never quit believing that I was good enough. No matter how many times the people who loved me, told me that I was talented and beautiful inside out, and that I mattered to them, I just wouldn't believe it.

I would pluck up the courage to apply for top jobs, for which I was qualified for and capable of doing, but somehow along the way I would lose my nerve and not follow through with the job application, which would pile up, until I finally plucked up the courage to apply again. I would only apply for something that I felt underqualified for as a safety net. However, when I did go all out, I would always be called for an interview, and I usually got the job. I was very good in interview situations, good with people.

My son is so much bolder than I. When applying for employment, he is fearless to this day. He would keep on submitting, right until he got a response, and like me, he is also very good at interviews and getting the job, and so much more. Sean is such an encourager. Anyone who genuinely comes in his presence, he encourages them to their fullest potential. Having Sean was the best thing that ever happened to me, aside from getting to know God. He was certainly God-sent. Sean is now married with a wife. a daughter and a son, who are his pride and joy, aside from God. He lives his life in a God-centred way, that makes me admire him more. He started his own business in catering, along with his wife, portraying their love, for good quality foods. The business got started approximately eight years ago, and has a good loyal staff comprised of family and friends. His business has growing by leaps and bounds since then. He encouraged his wife to pursue her degree, of which I believe she has several now, and helped to nurture her talents to a very high standard. I really love and admire my daughter in-law, Mercedes; she is a very talented loving mum, and I even call her super mum. Together with Sean, they are like a power couple, building each other up successfully. One of the things I admire in Sean even more is that when he is ready to put his mind to something, he goes all out to see it through and doesn't let up until he gets the job done. He has a good work ethic. To date, he is doing very well.

Before I had my son, my life was lonely, and I was constantly searching for love. Prior to having my son, I was always looking for love in the wrong places. So, I had my heart broken quite a few times, until I decided enough was enough. I had questions in my mind that I had no answers for. After years of never quite achieving all my goals, I was still searching for what was missing. Even after succeeding in academia, I was still looking for fulfilment in life.

CHAPTER XIII: The Devil's Counterfeit Husband against God's plans for your soulmate, your life

Before I came to know the Lord, I thought one time I found my soulmate in a man who I thought was my rock, because he gave me more than any relationship had. He seemed to be the one that I had been searching for all my life. He was very supportive and allowed me to live out some of my missed childhood dreams. He was so persistent when pursuing me I was flattered. He was also 17 years older than I was and I liked that he represented a father to me, which I never truly had. He made me feel secure, and he kind of grew on me.

Then he laid a bombshell on me when he told me that he was married. But by that time, I was in too deep. He convinced me that his marriage was over, so I said, "What do you want with me?". I had always made it a rule to leave married men alone, but he told me that he was in the process of getting a divorce from her. I asked him "What can you offer me?" He replied "Love, and money". I did like the idea of not having to worry over finance, as I was studying at university at the time, and he seemed to support that.

With certain reassurances from him, I decided to give the relationship a go. I even brought him home to meet my family; my family liked him very much, especially my brother Mervin, because he was easy to get along with. The relationship was getting serious, but within a few months, his wife found out, and decided on a plan of action. She was not going to let a young girl take her man away or live in what they had built together. They had three properties between them, and he decided to take two, which she put a stop to. So, he was left with one. Even then she was still not satisfied, she also wanted him dead. One night he was coming home from work, and he was attacked with a knife, almost losing his life. What I had gotten myself into, I thought. He was in the hospital for a while. After his discharge, he went to court but couldn't prove who attacked him.

We became engaged, and I was very happy. We cared for each other very much. After a while, I did wonder how I went from laughing at the little bald-headed old man to falling for him. Despite the jealousy over our relationship from some so-called friends, we just got on with our lives. We did some extensive renovations on our home.

Later, I found out that his wife was into the dark arts, but he insisted that he was not. I believed him, and also told him that I did not believe in those things. I did not think they would harm me; but ignorance is not always bliss! Then one day he told me that he felt his ex-wife was working black magic on him, and he wanted to go to Jamaica and sort her out. Ignorantly, I agreed to go with him to seek out a witch doctor to help him with his ex. Prior to that, however, he took me to visit his mother in the parish of St Thomas, which I was told had a large voodoo community. He obviously sought advice from his mother, who I believed was also heavily into the dark arts. Then I said I would like to visit my aunty in Mandeville, so he seemed to like the idea. After that, I am not sure what happened. I found myself asking one of my family members if he knew a witch doctor in the area. This just wasn't like me. So, we found one and I remember being very scared, but I told myself that I was doing this for my man. Upon our arrival he went in a little room, to be given some sort of a bath. Whatever happened, when he came out, he didn't seem himself. I was also given a bath and was told to drink some sort of a liquid, which was vile. The witch doctor told us to take this awful liquid back home and use it like perfume daily. I hated the vile thing, but I complied. All I know was that when we came back to England, nothing was ever the same. Instead of having a better relationship, it turned quickly sour. I couldn't for the life of me understand why. Our relationship just got worse, instead of better. We were on the verge of breaking up. Next thing, he wanted me out of our home. I thought that we would get married and that he would complete me. Instead, he turned into someone that I never knew; he was like a man possessed.

I was living in a nightmare, only I wasn't sleeping. When I look back, it wasn't real love. It was flaky and baseless. Then things just got from bad to worse when I think of how much of myself I put into the house. I just had to leave and I also had Sean to think of, so I couldn't just leave without anywhere to go. When Sean was still calling him 'dad', I was fuming, and I told Sean never to call him 'dad' again. Because my name was on the mortgage, he couldn't get me out so easily, so he would try to intimidate me. I also found out that he was seeing someone else, introduced to him by our next-door neighbour, who was also my cousin and one of those very jealous of our relationship. It came time for us to go to court over the property. Although I had friends in the know, who advised me to assert my right to the property, when it came to it I just couldn't. I told the court that I would give up my rights to the property, because he had lost his other properties to his ex-wife, I didn't want to take his only. And during that time, when I was still living in the spare room, he would come home and try to intimidate me. But I stood my ground. I also had my one long-time Christian friend looking out for me, and he would try to intimidate her also. He would tell her to get out, but she stuck by me, even sometimes staying the night, to ensure my safety. It was around that time, in my darkest hour, that I found the Lord. It was when the Lord gave me a promise of a new life in him, and a vision of his plan for my life, that I decided to leave the house.

He allowed me to take my share of the furniture, which I put in storage until I found a place to live. But as it happened, I ended up destroying all my furniture. Because I became ill and lost my mind, someone sent demons to attack me, and in my new home day and night I was always fighting demons, but I clung on to God's promise of deliverance. Even though I ended up losing all that I had in storage, I thought it was too material anyway. Thank God for my deliverance! The one thing that the Lord saved for me, out all my things, was my large mirror, because He meant me to see the real me in it.

CHAPTER XIV: Never call another human your rock, Jesus is your only Rock!

Looking back, I was so naive and so wrong about this man I give away my power to, and he used it against me. We had a huge break up; the rug was literally pulled from under me. I did not know what had hit me. One minute, this man was giving me anything I asked for, the next we were fighting in court over property/ I could not comprehend the change; it's like he was wearing a mask. Everything I thought I knew about him had suddenly been stripped away. This left me questioning my sanity, and self-worth. I was beside myself. I relied on him for so much that when we broke up, I had to relearn everything over again. I felt useless and helpless. It even made me harbour self-destructive thoughts. This is what happens when you live your life through people and not through God.

Human beings will always let you down, but God will never fail you. And it taught me another lesson: never call any human being your rock or look for a man to be your everything. God alone is your everything. Jesus is the only authentic rock in your life. God is a jealous God, and He will love you beyond your pain. This I found out the hard way. I remember mom saying one day that when I went to college I would find a husband'. Maybe that happened in the old days to some people for sure, but that certainly didn't happen to me.

Through it all, to continue in the aftermath of this relationship, I found out that it was not man that I needed but God. I would go down on my knees and pray to God to help me because I could no longer help myself. For the first time in my life, I felt lost. During those years, the Lord would always send his people my way, but I would not listen to them. God had to throw me flat on my face, so that I had nowhere to turn but to him. If He has to send you to prison, He will! Now I was ready to listen.

A good friend of mine would visit me and talk to me about her faith in God, then she would leave me with a leaflet, about having a relationship with Jesus. Jesus came when I felt reached, and I needed someone who I could trust. So, one night before I went to bed, I confessed to Jesus as my

Saviour. From then on, my life was never the same. The Lord led me to a church that was very big on confessing positive words over your life. And I flourished. I was introduced to prayer and fasting, which I took to very well.

One day, during my attempt to complete a 40 day fast, the Lord himself visited me in my room just 3 days into the fast. I had an old alarm clock at the bottom of my bed. Sometimes between morning and night, I was woken up by an immaculate white light surrounding the clock radio. I had never seen such a sight. As I sat up, it was showing 6.47 on the face of the clock. I did not fully understand what I had seen, so I laid back down. and though it is too early to wake up. I went back to sleep, and the Lord woke me up again, the clock still showing 6.47. So, I thought there cannot be two 6.47s in one morning, so I laid down again, and only this time the Lord clearly spoke to me, saying "Read Luke 6.47". So, I got up, still amazed that I heard from the Lord. In a daze, I picked up my Bible and turned to Luke, and it read:

"Whosoever cometh to me, and hearth my sayings, and doeth them, I will shew you to whom he is like: He is like a man which built a house, and dogged deep, and laid the foundation on a rock: and when the flood arose, the stream beat vehemently upon that house, and could not shake it: because it was founded upon the rock." (Luke 6.47)

That is the Rock, our Lord Jesus Christ. So, I locked at the scripture above and it said, "Why do you call me Lord, Lord, and do not the things which I say?" (Luke 6:46). When I looked further down the page, it said: "But he that hearth, and doeth not, is like a man that without a foundation built his house upon the earth; against [i.e. the world, life gets in the way] which the streams did beat vehemently, and immediately it fell; and the ruin of that house was great" (Luke 6:49).

I remember I couldn't wait to go to church and tell my Pastor what the Lord has said. I was so excited, when I told my Pastor, and she seemed so pleased to hear it. I thought all Christians had that vision of the Lord. But later I was to realis, every Christian, has their own vision and story to tell.

Verse 46 is saying that when God tells us to do something, we listen but we don't do it, and in the next prayer we are asking Him to do something for us, and we expect Him to do it. Then verses 47 and 48 tell you that when you do what God tells you to do, there is nothing He wouldn't do for you, and he will make your enemies to be your footstool, and you will forever be in his divine protection and favour. However, verse 49 says, if you do not answer his call, nothing you do in life will be fulfilling and all your labour will be in vain, and your soul will be eternally loss.

CHAPTER XV: A Locked Heart

When I came to the Lord, I had so much hurt, with unforgiveness, anger, and resentment, which I turned inwardly on myself. I felt so rejected, used, and abused, stemming from what I had been through in my life, and from past relationships. A family friend was so jealous of me that she tried to kill me by putting poison in my food and also working black magic on me. When she first visited my home, she couldn't believe her eyes. According to her I had too much, a good man, a big house, and top qualification. I was so shocked, at what she tried to do to me. It knocked me for six, and basically she wanted everything I had to be handed to her, and then she wanted me dead. Man's jealousy is as cold as the grave, so please don't underestimate a person who is jealous of you. Take it seriously because it can lead to murder. She obviously saw me as more successful than I saw myself. I felt so used and abused. But I hid it well. People always saw me as someone who had it all together. But that was not the case.

I am a naturally shy person, and I used to hide my pain by being the life and soul of the party. I used to chatter non-stop, so that no one would realise how shy and insecure I really was. If someone spotted my shyness, I would deny it, by saying I am happy go lucky, I am a bubbly and cheerful person. I very rarely showed anyone the real me. I was hiding the fact that I did not like myself, that I was never happy with my weight. I was only happy with myself when I lost weight. So, I continued on a never-ending quest to be slim, on one diet to another, always searching for a quick fix. I did not want to admit that I was a yoyo dieter. I always found it easy to lose weight, but keeping it off was the challenge.

I don't think that there is any diet that I had not been on. As soon as I finished one diet and got to my goal, all I had to do was eat normally, and the weight would pile back on. It is not as if I was a massive eater. My metabolism was messed up from all the abuse through food from a young age, starvation one minute and overfeeding the next by those in Jamaica who were meant to take care of me. The whole process was so stressful. I remember I used to be envious of slim people, because they seem to have it all together, but that is not necessary the case. When you try to eat like them, it does not always work out because most of them eat like you anyway. They just burn it of quicker, and because your system is very different, you just can't compare. Sometimes genes play a part. That is why you can't get some of them to understand why you have weight problems. They think that you just overeat, which is not the same issue for everybody. For some, there are medical issues, so you can't always judge a book by the cover Only someone with the same issues as you can truly understand.

I began to believe that people only liked me when I was slim, and some actually did. I certainly got more attention, when I was slim. So many of us hide deep hurt behind a mask, which we put on daily, just like applying makeup, and remove it sometimes behind closed doors, depending on who you live with. We erect barriers, to stop people getting close enough to hurt us again. We are so puffed up and full of pride. I used to be one of them, and the Lord would sometimes ask me why I was so puffed up. Then I would smile and ask the Lord to forgive me for being puffed up.

But know that pride comes before a fall. I thank God that I am not where I used to be.

There was a time I used to worry about anything and everything, I would call myself a professional worrier. I had so much negative thoughts going round in my head, that for a period I just couldn't think for myself anymore, and a loving friend had to think for me. I felt that my mind was a blank box. I remember one day, when I was studying for my degree, I had to completely clear my mind of all the different negative emotions, primarily about my family, that came to the surface, preventing me from focusing on my studies. I had to block them out, hold them down, in order to pass my exam, which I did successfully. But I just did not realise how emotionally damaged I was. I locked my emotions in a vault in my heart, thinking that they, had completely gone, but they were still hiding beneath the surface, waiting to be unearthed.

Further down the line, these locked emotions attacked me with a vengeance in the form of depression. It was a shock to my system because I was always able to pick myself up in the past when I fell. I found that I just couldn't cope with life anymore; I felt like a lost little girl. But I realised that I had a young son to take care of, so I had to keep on going for him. I had to be well enough in order to help him become a high achiever and the best version of himself that he could be. Later on, when the bottom of my world fell out, I became homeless, and felt destitute.

CHAPTER XVI: Be wary of fair-weather friends

I went to a Christian friend, named Jill, who I thought was a true friend. I got to know her, because the Lord sent her along with two other Christian ladies to my house to pray for me in my darkest hour. Through that we built up a friendship, which I thought was strong. We were always in each other's company, visiting different churches and generally having a laugh together, but I was wrong. When I became homeless, and arrived at her house with Sean, I told her that the Lord told me to come. I saw that she didn't look happy about it, apparently. She had a male lodger, so I did not realise how unwelcomed Sean and I were. In the middle of the night, the lodger came to me and gave me both barrels. He then proceeded to tell me all he knew about my life, and what a mess I made of it. He told me all about my wrong relationships, in a very embellished and colourful way, with lies added. I felt like I was hit by a heavy goods vehicle. I felt so confused and betrayed by my friend Jill. Of course, I defended myself, but he wanted me out there and then. Then realisation dawned: he was more than a lodger, he was a lodger with benefits. I got up and ran out the door, knowing I had nowhere to go. I couldn't take Sean with me; he was too young to be woken out of his sleep so late at night. So, I left him, to come back for him in the morning. I ended up in Croydon Town Centre on a bench, and that was where I spent the night, because I was miles away from my other friends, who I know would have taken me in. When I went back to take Sean, I saw Jill briefly, but I was so hurt and angry at her for betraying my trust that I just left without saying a word.

The Lord led me to Erona, a very loyal friend, who made a place in her home for us, as long as we needed it. It is at times like these, that you know who your true friends are. She did all the thinking for me because I couldn't think for myself anymore. I will always be eternally grateful to my dear friend Erona. She took us in even though there was so much opposition; she stood firmly in my corner. That's not to say that my other friends weren't supportive, because I now realise that the Lord had been choosing my friends from the very beginning. My other good friends played their part in my life by giving me so much love and support. Still today, we are all good friends.

No matter how long we are apart, whether weeks, months, or years, when we meet up, it is as if we only saw each other yesterday. The Lord knew how much I needed the right people around me.

Going back to Jill, I kept away from her for several years. I was so hurt that I had to forgive her over and over again until the anger left me. When we did see each other again, I tried to tell her what her lodger/boyfriend said to me, but I could see that no matter what I said, it was not going to go down well. However, she listened and said she would speak to him. Eventually, we agreed to differ, and because I didn't want to hold onto unforgiveness, I had to forgive them. A few years later, I rang her and told her that I was getting married, and I wanted her to come. Immediately, she told me that she was also going to be married. I was so surprised, and of course I was even more surprised to hear she was getting married to the lodger, of course. She actually got married before me; it was as if, because I told her that I was getting married, she had to beat me to the altar. A few years elapsed, and we tried to keep up a sort of friendship. I began working as a Retail Manager and would invite her to the store now and again to buy some outfits, and I would even help her out with my staff discount, still trying to prove to myself that I had forgiven them.

After a while, I stopped trying so hard. She would ring me, but the calls weren't productive. Other times, I wouldn't answer, and eventually she got the message. More years went by, and our lives took different turns. I went to visit her out of the blue one day because I felt the Lord told me so. During our greetings, we told each other what we had been doing with our lives. I proceeded to tell her that I was writing my autobiography. She immediately asked if she was in it with trepidation. Until she said that, I hadn't even thought of putting her in it. I knew if I mentioned her, she would not fare well.

Now I realise that she is actually a big part of my story to this day. She had two children, a boy and a girl, from a previous marriage. When I heard that her daughter had recently died, in 2021, I was so sad, because she was lovely, just a little older that Sean. Sean and I were very fond of them; they were part of our life for so long, like family. I rang her to express my condolences, but she was very cold towards me. I just put that down to her grief. I asked her if Sean and I could attend the funeral; she agreed, but begrudgingly. However, when the day came, and I was too sick to go. I asked Sean and his wife to go instead and explain why I couldn't come, because I genuinely wanted to attend. When Sean came home, I asked him how it went, he said she was so cold towards them, barely introducing them to anyone. He felt uncomfortable, left early, and couldn't find the opportunity to explain why I couldn't come. So, I took it upon myself to phone her to explain to her, that I genuinely wanted to come but was unwell. Still, I only got coldness from her. I guess some friends are only temporarily in your life for God's purpose. The Lord says, "Cast your worries upon Him because He, cares for you..." (1 Peter 5:7). So I did just that.

Another fair-weather friend was Claudia. Claudia was a Christian girl I met when I started my first job. She was much older than I was and seemed to be very wise, so I looked up to her, like an older sister. We would spend many lunch hours chatting about one thing or another. She would make me feel so at ease, so I trusted her with my life story. I told her about what happened to me in Jamaica, and the way my mom treated me here, and how unhappy I was when I lived at home, so we continued with our friendship. Then I eventually left work to further my education. Then years later we met up again, and the first thing she said was that her sister met my mom through work, and it came about that they got talking and found out that I was friends with Claudia. All that I had told Claudia was relayed to her sister, which was then relayed to mom, who denied everything and made me out to be a liar. No surprise there. Straight away, Claudia believed everything my mom said, and told me my mom is a nice lady so everything I said was a lie. Sometimes people are quicker to believe a lie than the truth. Anyway, I was so shocked and disappointed after enjoying the close friendship I thought we had. It was not real. When I tried to defend myself, she would not listen to me and brushed me aside. That was very hurtful.

Another thing she told me that really hurt me was when I told her that I had finally become a Christian like her, and how the Lord was positively working through me. I thought she would be pleased, but she just said people like me only came to the Lord when in trouble. She said nothing positive, and she just continued her negativity about why I became a Christian. So, I remained disappointed. I held my peace, buried my hurt for a few years without seeing her. When I met up with her again, my anger, hurt and unforgiveness showed itself in my cold greetings to her. She probably wondered what was wrong. Some people do and say things that hurt others because they don't think before they speak, and because they too are hiding hurt, but there is a saying: those who feel it knows it.

Then the Lord told me that I must forgive her. This was hard to hear, but I began to pray for her and ask the Lord to help me to forgive. This included phoning her and ironing out the whole thing. She was surprised, because she couldn't believe that I had held on to this thing for so long. But this is what some of us do, when we feel betrayed and have been hurt deeply. We believe that we can deal with it ourselves, but all we end up doing is burying it. But God will dig it up and bring it out in the open, for our own good, because He is the Master grave digger. Believe me, holding on to unforgiveness is not worth the effort and pain it costs to hold on to it. So, let it go and let God in. As previously stated, God only puts some people in your life for a short time. If you try to keep them any longer, you will be disappointed. Joyce Meyer wrote a piece in one of her daily readings, saying

"Anyone who needs emotional healing, and restoration from past hurt must learn to face truth. We cannot be set free while living in denial. If you are hurt, talk to God about it openly, because He cares about anything that concerns you. Many times, people who have suffered abuse or some other tragedy, in their lives, try to act as though it never happened. Early traumatic experiences can cause us to be emotionally damaged and wounded later in life because we develop opinions and attitudes about ourselves based on what happened to us".

Sometimes the meanest people are hurting the most inside. She goes on to say:

"The day came when I realized, I had to face the truth and stop pretending. It is when we truly open our hearts and let God work in our lives, that we can become what God wants us to be, when all those layers of pretence that we have heaped up over the years, are stripped away, only then can we truly be free and happy to enjoy the person God made us to be".

It is as if she was speaking directly to me, when I was going through my trials. I did not know how to feel, so I just pretended to be happy, then I would hide my hurt. But what I do remember, was that the healing process felt more rigorous than what I had been through, because God had to dig so deep to resurrect all that I had hidden and buried for years. But I thank God for being a God of restoration.

When we allow unforgiveness in our lives, we are filled with resentment and bitterness that can lead to so many other negative emotions, detrimental to our health. The Bible refers to it as something that is pungent or sharp, like the Passover meal that included bitter herbs to remind the Israelites of their long years of captivity in Egypt. This means we need to be long suffering, and transparent, if we want God's best in our lives. No-one wants to eat bitter herbs all their lives, do they?

I remember one day saying to myself I was going to be more like these aggressive people who have no filter. They just open their mouths without caring what they say or how it affects other people. They would just speak plainly. So, I tried doing the same, but I found that after a while, I had lost myself and I couldn't remember who I was. I just became more closed off, unforgiving, and filled with resentment towards the people who hurt me along the way. But instead of letting it go, I would internalize it and cover it up with a smile or a cheerful countenance. Deep down, I was aching and crying inside, but little did I realize what it was doing to my system, and my internal organs. I thank God that He did not allow me to get to the bitter stage. Believe me, holding on to anger and bitterness is hard going. As previously stated, it takes a great effort to hold on to hate, and it can lead you to doing something you may later regret. The diagnosis of the Great Physician in the sky, is to let it go, and be free from your infirmity, and live a complete life. In the end you are only hurting yourself.

Like myself, some of us bury our hurt feelings and live our life behind a mask so that we don't have to deal with these emotions, but they are still there, only sleeping, waiting to be unearthed and confronted. Sometimes we don't even realise that they are still there because they are down so deep, but keep on trusting the Master grave digger and his electric shovel to bring them to the surface. And believe me, the Lord knows when you are ready. Bottling up our feelings will only make us ill. God wants us to live balanced, complete lives somewhere between where we are, and where He wants us to be. We still need to think before we speak, and speak with love.

CHAPTER XVII: I was lost and in a haze of unfilled desires and disappointments

Years later, it took my relationship with God to find myself again. The Lord showed me that He made me to be kind, loving and compassionate, and to have integrity. This is hard to do in this world and with some people in your life, and especially without God at the helm. He showed me that He wants me to be the best version of myself that I can be. He did not create us to be anyone else. In order for me to achieve this, I had to forgive. Forgiveness brings healing and restoration. It brings positive changes in your life, and brings joy to your soul. In other words, God wants us to enjoy everyday life. When Peter, one of Jesus's disciples, asked Jesus, "Lord, how oft shall my brother sin against me, and I forgive him? till seven times? Jesus saith unto him, I say not unto thee, Until seven times: but, Until seventy times seven" (Matthew 18:21). In other words, infinity. Just as the Lord has infinitely forgiven us without conditions.

When you don't forgive, you hold yourself in bondage to all those people that you won't forgive, and that in turn affect your whole body. It can, I believe, affect your heart, leading to heart attack, kidney and liver failure, and can also affect the digestive system and your mental psyche. In fact, it will affect your wellbeing. And when your well-being or mental health is affected, this can lead in some extreme cases to suicidal thoughts and acts. Our bodies were not meant to maintain worry or stress. That's why Jesus says to cast our cares upon Him and he will give us rest. Then, He showed me that holding on to unforgiveness is like taking a bottle of poison and drinking it yourself while thinking it will affect the other person. The Bible says "Fret not yourself about evildoers…" (Psalm 37:1). In many places in the Bible He says not to worry or fear. "Casting all your care upon him; for he careth for you" (1 Peter 7) […] "for my yoke is easy and my burden is light" (Matthew 11:30). Because Jesus experiences all that we go through and much more.

It took years for me to understand this, and for the Lord to deliver me, and work on my self-esteem. It was bittersweet, sometimes more bitter than sweet. But the Lord strengthened me and carried me through. He showed me that I did not love myself, and that I was hurting inside. So, He began to work on me. He got me to look in the mirror and confess self-love and acceptance, because He loves and accepts me, just as I am. However, my journey as a new Christian was very hard. I met some good people along the way and some not so good, but the Lord still kept me. I remember thinking that all Christians were to be trusted, but I found out to my cost that wasn't always the case. People were still people and are therefore subject to human failings. We all share some of the same struggles, so I still had to choose my friends wisely. When I was at the height of my battles, I gave my power away to the wrong people, thinking that they would be able to help me, because their lives seemed more together than mine. But I met with more disappointments. All that meant was that I was more honest about my struggles than they were, and I had to learn that the hard way. But you know, it is good to be found in God. If I had not experienced loss, I wouldn't know what 'found' feels like.

One of the things I learned was that hurting people hurt people. As I said before, man will lie to you, but God will not. Because man sees the outward appearance, but God sees the heart. Human beings can say what they want you to hear, and you have to believe, until you see different. When you can do bad things, and hide it from people, you cannot hide your stuff from God. God will always be true to you because He is a good and faithful God, and He cannot lie. His promises are always true. I thank God that He was the one constant hope I had in my life, even when I didn't know Him. He loved me unconditionally, and He used my son to help keep me grounded and happy. Having a little person to take care of, who would not Judge me, was just the tonic I needed. Because of my own bad experience, I made sure that my son did not go through the same experience that I had been through. So, I set about building him up with positive words. He never heard me say anything that was less than positive about his character throughout his life.

As a child I was constantly told that I was not good enough, not good looking enough, not the right shade, too fat, or that I would never amount to anything, if I didn't act in a certain way. After a while I began to believe it, and then I would begin to act it out, but then sometimes I would tell myself I am not going to do to another person what was done to me. Sometimes the very same person responsible for your heart's torment comes from the same abused situation themselves, and therefore cannot do any better. The devil never attacks you in one go, he works on you over time, because he sees and knows your potential. Then he begins to work towards assassinating your character from the get-go.

God had a plan for my life. It wasn't until I was in my forties that I fully realised that God had a plan for my life and that He had to bring me to a certain place in order to achieve it. I needed to accept His love and also love myself. I used to always think that I was married to Jesus and didn't need an earthly husband. God had a husband tailor made for me, but I missed out on that because I chose wrongly for myself when I wasn't completely healed, and therefore not hearing correctly. So, I misheard what God was saying, even when my Pastor intervened. People knew it was too soon because of the trauma I suffered from my past relationship. Because I believed that God chose my husband for me, I did not listen to His warnings. I was so stubbornly sure that my husband was a Godsend, and I would not allow anyone to tell me any different.

CHAPTER XVIII: I met Darren

I was introduced to my husband by a newly acquainted work colleague who said that she knew a nice Christian man that she would like to introduce me to. She thought we would make a good match. I was sceptical at first, to say the least, so I said no. However, after some weeks had passed, I began to have a change of heart. I said to myself, 'Angela, why did you say no? What if this woman is the vehicle that God has chosen to give you a husband? What if you miss out on God's best for you? You owe it to yourself to find out if he is the one!'. So, I went back to my friend and told her that I changed my mind. I even got a little impatient waiting for her to get back to me. Then I started to get a little excited about the outcome.

We met on a blind date. Although we talked on the phone a little, we hadn't met up yet. When we did finally meet, the chemistry between us was undeniable. We hit it off straight away. My husband is a very sociable person, and he always has something to say. And when I found out that he had the same birthday as one of my closest

135

friends, that gave me more reassurance that he was the one. I felt that God would iron out any flaws in his character, so I felt it was important to be up front with Darren from the get-go. I wasn't looking for a causal relationship. I am a child of God, and I love my Lord, and I will obey Him at all costs. So, it is marriage or nothing. I saw his thoughts going around in his mind, thinking about what I said. After a while, he seemed to have come to a decision, and so we continued dating. I invited him around to meet my son, who seemed to like him too. I know Sean longed for a father figure.

I remember one day saying to Darren that he was getting too overbearing, because he was getting too full on. But the more I tried to break it off with him, the more he would find any excuse to come around and do Jobs that I needed done around the house. He kind of made himself indispensable, so I got to like his persistence, and also his bulldozing ways, which I now don't like about him and did not realise then could be abusive. He just seemed strong and dependable, what I thought I needed at the time, and the fact that Sean liked him gave me hope, so I ignored the red flags.

Finally, after a short courtship, Darren surprised me with a marriage proposal. I was so surprised. Although I had told him directly it was marriage or nothing, I never believed that he would actually propose. He came to visit me one day. Sean was in the front room watching TV and we were in the kitchen talking. Then all of a sudden Darren went down on one knee and proposed to me. I guess I was so caught up in the fairy-tale moment of it. Of course, I said a great big fat yes. He thought we would get married in a registry office, but I wasn't having that. I made it clear that I wanted a Church wedding, or no wedding at all. I asked the Lord for a fairy-tale wedding, and that is what I was going have, so he reluctantly agreed. We were to be married on the 19th September 1998. In reality, I don't think either of us were madly in love, but the attraction was very strong. And I thought, if I did not have successful relationships with people that I knew over a long period in the past, I might as well give this short courtship a go because we certainly got on well. And from that I thought love would surely grow. And it did.

However, when my pastor heard the news, he invited me to his home for the talk because he was not happy with my choice. He spent the whole day asking me what I knew about Darren's background. I told him that he had two sons living in Jamaica. He said I shouldn't be marrying someone who has already got two children, and unmarried. My reply was that I also had one son and I was unmarried. He said that was beside the point and continued with his rhetoric about Darren's unsuitability as a husband. He said that my healing was still ongoing, and this could set me back big time. I could see that what he said was coming from a good place, but I thought that he did not know Darren as I did. So, his opinion was biased. I looked to his wife for validation, but she just smiled without getting involved. So, I proceeded angrily to tell my pastor that I would go ahead and marry Darren because I believe God sent him to me. From that point, he gave up saying anything more to me. From then on, any pastor that told me anything negative about my proposed marriage to Darren, I would not listen to them because my mind was already made up, and I was still reeling from what I saw as my pastor's interference in my life.

When we eventually found a pastor to marry us, I remember our first meeting with Pastor Powell.

He was very kind and non-judgmental. He even encouraged us to have some counselling beforehand. I remember him saying, 'Teeth and tongue will have to meet.' But I also remember being too scared that I would find that Darren and I were unsuited, so I ignored Pastor Powell's advice. I guess I just wanted to get married. With hindsight, I wished I had listened to my pastor's advice. The wedding got underway, and I remember one of my work colleagues offering to gift me all of the bridal flowers, which were very expensive, and other people, some acquaintances, some friends and family, would contribute in other ways. I felt blessed. The wedding day dawned, and I was so pleased and surprised to see my old pastor and the members of his church in attendance. All was forgiven. I think he was surprised to see how well attended and classy the wedding was. Although our marriage would last more than twenty-five years, we would have many trials along the way.

Chapter XIX: Prior to meeting Darren

Before meeting my Darren, I used to make regular visits to a friend who lived in Crystal Palace. On the bus journey to call on my friend, each time the bus passed Crystal Palace Bridal Shop, I would find myself looking at the bridal dresses. One day, there was one which particularly caught my eye: a 1920s / 1930s riding dress with top hat and a veil. I just fell in love with it. This was possibly nearly about a year before I met my Darren, and each time I visited my friend, I would wonder why I kept on looking at this one bridal dress, when there was not the least thought that marriage would be on the cards for me. I thought I was going crazy or something.

So, as soon as Darren proposed, I knew exactly where I was going to get my wedding dress. I took this to be another sign. I asked one of my best friends to come with me, and she also agreed that this was my dress. It stood out from the rest. I even tried going to go to a few other bridal shops, but I just couldn't get the first dress out of my mind. It was such a beautiful designer dress in my favourite green and ivory colours.

I now believe that the Lord knew that I was going to marry hastily from the beginning, but because of my faithfulness to Him, He honoured my marriage anyway. I certainly was not financially prepared for marriage. At this time, I couldn't even afford my dress, which I wanted to purchase for myself. So, I told Darren about how much I loved the dress, and straight away he gave me the money to pay for it. Darren can be generous when he wants to be. Darren also took over the organizing of the whole wedding like a pro wedding planner. All I could do was sit back and watch him. He did such a good job; I was impressed as he just took the stress of the planning off me.

Our wedding went so well, almost exactly the way I wanted it, with a few exceptions. And the fact that Darren accomplished the organising in a short space of time made me admire him even more. I asked the Lord for sunshine on my day, and He gave it. Almost all that I prayed for came to pass. He gave me sunshine on what was normally a rainy, cold and gloomy September month. Even more reasons for me to believe that Darren was the right partner for me. When a few well-meant people questioned my relationship, I would say God choose my husband and I genuinely believe this. I ignored my anxiety, and deep-seated doubt. I allowed Darren to convince me that we belonged together. And for all intents and purposes, Darren appeared to be the one. I remember my brother Mervin saying, as we stood together at the Church door waiting for me to be walked me down the aisle, 'It's not too late to back out now, sis!'. My response was, 'I want this!'. I guess in the end people saw how happy we were and, supported us. When we got married, everybody said that this was the best wedding they had ever been to and that it was a marriage made in heaven. That just confirmed to me that God was in this.

From then on, everything that Darren tried to accomplish, he did. The areas where he wasn't so strong, I encouraged him. I stood beside him every step of the way. We seemed to balance each other out. I remember one of my friends said that she had prayed to God for a husband for me. Later on, down the line, she said that she asked the Lord why He gave me a husband and not her, to which the Lord replied I needed love. God's mercy kept me. God knew the sincerity of my heart, and in grace and mercy kept me. He blessed my marriage anyway.

My husband Darren was blessed through our marriage, but I did not feel blessed. The Bible says, "Anyone who finds a wife finds a good thing and receives blessings from the Lord" (Proverbs 18:22). As for myself, I couldn't see the blessings. I had so many unfulfilled desires which were plaguing me. So, the devil would torment me with thoughts like 'God has nothing for you'. 'What is He doing for you?', 'Your husband is getting so much blessing; what can you show, through your close walk with him?', 'You have all these qualifications and talents; why is God not allowing you to use them and make you a success?'. But sometimes we wait when we should act, because of fear of failure and lack of trust in God. God will never give you more than you can bear. Even when we are disobedient, we are in God's waiting room.

Darren and I have very different personalities and temperaments. He let his feelings out, at whatever the cost, while I keep my feelings in so as not to offend, even when I am offended. I am a two-word person, and I don't feel the need to be loud and over the top. But my husband knew which buttons to push, to get me to react. But God kept me through it all. One of the things I admire about Darren is that together we both had good work ethics, which we passed on to our sons. Darren, an electrician by trade, was also very good at DIY. He could turn his hand to any form of manual labour successfully, and also had a very good head for maths. We both worked very hard to give our children a good start in life. Because our children saw how hard we worked to take care of them, they in turn learned to stand up to their responsibilities.

As a single parent I did my best with my childcare responsibilities, and I am very proud of my accomplishments. But the Word also says, "That if two of you shall agree on earth as touching anything that they shall ask, it shall be done for them of my Father which is in heaven. For where two or three are gathered together in my name, there am I in the midst of them" (Matthew 19:20). So having two parents to show you how the world works can only be a good thing. The added bonus I gained through my marriage is two lovely stepsons who now also have children and businesses of their own. I am very glad to be part of their lives.

God holds us together with His divine glue. So, regardless of the fact that I jumped into marriage too soon instead of waiting on God, He was still merciful. He held us together, with His divine glue, through the good times and the bad. God saw me through a lot of turbulent years in my marriage. However, after twenty or more years, Darren and I separated a couple of times. First, for a couple of months, then we got back together thinking things would change. Another time we separated for 6 months. I had had enough after years of verbal abuse at his hands. It took me a long time to realise that I was in an abusive relationship. I kept making excuses for his behaviour, telling myself that God will change him and asking God to change me instead. No matter what he did or said to my detriment, I would blame myself, especially because I couldn't get him to admit fault. I would internalise my pain because I had control only over my own emotions, so it was easier to take the blame. But by meditating on the word of God, I strengthened myself in every area of my life including my self-esteem. One of the books I found myself constantly meditating on, was 'The Tongue: a Creative force', published by Charles Capps in 1970.

Time spent away from my marital home made me finally see what I was allowing another person to do to me, so I stopped blaming myself. My mental health had really suffered over the years. It took 22 odd years of putting up with Darren's verbal abuse to finally see that I was allowing him to project all his own negative feelings about himself onto me, and I would believe him. Even though I knew the truth, in the process, I lost myself again. I could only see myself in a negative light but God kept giving me his healing balm.

I came to realise that I spent our entire marriage building Darren up, but he spent the same amount of time tearing me down in order to make himself feel good. I found myself again through prayers and supplication. Darren lost himself for a while, during my absence. After a while we began to correspond. He wanted us to get back together, but I didn't want that. I was enjoying my freedom too much. So, I told him the only way I would go back to him was through genuine change, that only God could bring. So, no amount of promises or threats he made would make me change my mind. I wonder why I did not leave him sooner. I realised that I spent too long in denial, pretending that everything was alright, when in reality I was unhappy in my marriage and my mental health suffered in the process.

But do you know what I really realised during my time apart? I had placed Darren as head of the house literally, but not many men can live up to that responsibility. Some men cannot manage the responsibility of being head of the home. They may want and crave the title, but when it comes to them stepping up, they end up stepping down. Many of us women go looking for a real man, but what we find is a weak man pretending to be strong.

However, it took my leaving Darren to start to seeing genuine change in him. As I saw him draw closer to God, he actually apologised to me in front of our Church members. That made him attractive to me again. Then a little while after, he got very sick with COVID, and I found myself having to nurse him back to health because he couldn't do anything for himself. Through all of that, we ended up getting back together again after months apart, something I swore I would never do again. But once again, after a while, promises were made and broken on and off. So here we go again on that same old treadmill. Things were not as bad as they had been, but they were certainly not the way they should be. However, I was not putting up with what I used to, because I love myself far too much now to allow anyone's opinion of me to dictate my actions or my life. So, I have just left everything in God's hands.

CHAPTER XX: Abusers never want to be exposed

Within the confines of marriage, many abuses are not spoken about. Abusers never want to be outed, so they make all kinds of promises or threats, to keep you from speaking out. So, we put on the perfect front to keep up appearances, pretending we have the perfect relationship. Sometimes, it's out of fear of reprisal from our partners or for fear of being alone, or due to economic necessities, or shame of letting people know what you are really going through. And again, when children are involved, they also get hurt in the crossfire. God wants us to live happy, healthy, wholesome lives in Him, so stop pretending. Let God help you.

Never give away your power to another human being. I repeat a lot of my problems stemmed from freely giving away my power to people with the belief that I wasn't good enough, that they were better able to handle adversity than I had been. I had very little confidence in my own judgment and ability until God showed me who He made me to be; I am continuing to grow in him.

Mom used to say, 'Go to college and you would find a husband.' But that didn't happen for me. I was always looking for that knight in shining armour to take charge, complete me and make decisions for me, because I believed that I was not good enough, or capable enough to make informed decision. I also found it very easy to encourage others to their fullest potential but I found it hard to encourage myself. I found it much easier to put myself down. I was brought up to believe that men were the stronger sex and should be in charge. Some of that is true, but women are multi-functional and talented, who not only play a supportive and functional role within the family but also work very hard outside the home, to help supplement the family income. There used to be a lot of 'I can't' in my vocabulary, but now my vocabulary is 'yes' and 'amen'. We all have to work out our own salvation in this life; no one can do it for you. The Lord showed me that I did not know my own strength.

Just when we think that we can't, or will never, make it, Jesus shows up, telling us that we can. I now know, "I can do all things through Christ which strengtheneth me" (Philippians 4:11) [...]

Because Jesus has overcome the world and even all our faith (John 16:33). Jesus has deprived the world, Satan, of its power to harm us, so we need to stop allowing the cares of this world to deprive us of our happiness and wellbeing, and receive God's love and peace. When we choose peace, we choose the Prince of Peace, who is always available to us through the Holy Spirit, because He lives inside of you. It is absolutely amazing what we can accomplish in Christ if we make Him our Lord and Saviour, and just live one day at a time in him. He says "My grace is sufficient for you" (2 Corinthians 12:9).

When we harbour unforgiveness in our hearts, roots of bitterness can spring up through unresolved issues with people in the past. Unforgiveness is a root from which everything that is bad springs from. People who refuse to forgive are bitter, angry, feel guilty, rejected, abandoned, or outraged. We also need to forgive ourselves for making wrong decisions, or poor choices in life. When we don't, the symptoms we display, and can be dire to our mental health.

We must allow God to get in on the inside of us to dig that root of unforgiveness out so that we can have a healthy, happy life. And when we forgive, that temptation to commit suicide, or anything detrimental to our health, is diminished. We cannot bring our own justice, if we have been mistreated. Only God is just. He will deal with your enemies once you stop hating and start loving and forgive. And after that God will bring us emotional healing. But we have to want it, and we have to let him.

Believe me, accepting that we need to change is not easy because we are so prideful. We want people to think that we have everything together. Some of us want you to believe that, what you see is what you get, but that is not always the case. We have to render ourselves vulnerable to God, warts and all. My change certainly did not come easily; it was a slow and painful process, because I had so many demons of unforgiveness, abandonment and disappointment down to my roots, which God had to dig up. Wrong words spoken over the course of my life, by others or by myself, and I had to forgive myself. Words are like weapons. they sometimes wound, or they can make well. God had to first uncover them openly. He had to show me that I had to change my way of thinking and acting, that I had to trust Him to work on me.

God used a good friend and strong prayers to open me up and get me to talk about my life. I fought this friend every step of the way; it was so painful to talk about what I had been through. The pain was so visible and uncomfortable. It was like I was tearing myself apart myself. I had to undergo three or more years of intense deliverance to get me to a reasonable standard and begin the healing process. First, I had to go to all those people that I felt hurt me the most and forgive them and ask them to forgive me. Even when I did not feel that I was in the wrong, I asked God why. He said that it was for my benefit, to begin my healing. I was not to trouble myself if they didn't say anything back; Je will deal with them, and so I did what the Lord asked me to do. However, thankfully, I did not need to go to everybody, that would be too long and costly. So, I just began to ask the Lord to help me forgive all those people who I was not able for one reason or another to go to physically.

CHAPTER XXI: The Lord is asking, 'do you want to be made whole'?

From that day, my prayer always consisted of:

> *Dear Lord, I forgive all those who have sinned against me. By faith in your word, I choose to forgive, heal my emotions.*

Even when I didn't feel like it, and believe me, if I went by my feelings, I wouldn't do it because some people are hard to forgive. But I trusted God to do His part. The other part of my prayer was always:

> *Dear Lord, I pray that if anyone has unforgiveness towards me soften their hearts towards me.*

Ultimately, forgiveness is an act of faith. The word says, "if we forgive each other, our trespasses, the Lord will forgive us." (Matthew 6:14-15). I had to understand that if I wanted to be healed and made whole, I had to be obedient to God's word, whether I feel like it or not.

Forgiving someone who has wronged you is an act of faith.

And when you act in obedience to God's leading, you will be amazed at what He does in your life. Remember, forgiveness is not a feeling; it is a decision. You will find that sometimes, when you have forgiven that person in private, then when you see them in public, all the old feelings resurface, and you wander if you have forgiven them or want to. Don't think negative; just keep on praying for them, and keep the faith. Trust God and He will work it out for you. Just act normal with that person, let them marvel at your kindness towards them. "What you do in secret, the Lord will reward you openly". (Matthew 6:4)

I am not saying that this is easy, certainly not, but just do it, and you will see God transform your lives. Sometimes we hold people up in our hearts and don't know it. Remember God sees the heart; man sees the outward appearance. So, in prayer, always ask God:

Dear Lord, if I have unforgiveness in my heart towards anyone [your spouse, or even a close family member, or your closest friend],

158

please bring them to mind so that I
can forgive them.'

And He will bring them to your mind there and then. No matter how many times, just keep on forgiving them.

Let me say this again. Sometimes it is easier to forgive some people more than others; it depends on how deep the wound is. But look at what they did to Jesus; yet He still forgave them, and believe me, He forgives us in, seconds, minutes, hourly, daily and so on. Even when He was suffering and dying on the cross, and when He was mocked by the people, He still cried "Father, forgive them, for they know not what they do.". He even showed compassion to one of the two thieves crucified beside Him when He asked for forgiveness. Believe me, He is still in the business of forgiving today. How awesome, wonderful He is.

The Minister and Author Joyce Meyer, in one of her studies, quotes the scriptures from John 5:5-6 and says the below:

"There was a certain man who had suffered with a deep seated and lingering condition/disorder, for 38 years. When Jesus noticed him lying there, helpless, knowing that he had been in that same condition for a long time, He said to him, 'Will you be made whole? Do you really want to get well?' Because you have to want to. We have a saying in the world. You can lead a horse to water, but you can't force him to drink it. The Lord is asking you and me that same question today, 'Will you be made whole?' For 38 years long, this man has been waiting for his healing, perhaps half-heartedly until Jesus passed by. Do you know that there are people who don't want to get well; and prefer to talk to anyone, who would listen to them about their problems?'

I remember when I was working in a hospital, I heard of patients who visited the hospital every day about one complaint or another. They were so regular that you began to know them by sight and name. Sometimes it is for comfort and reassurance. Some of us wear our ailments and problems like a badge of honour as our identity, defying anyone to have a worse complaint than they have.

What a good thing that the Lord did not specify the nature of the thorn in Paul's side when he talks about his ailment. God did not specify what ailment he had, because the competition would really begin. God gives all his people their own thorn to keep them on their knees and keep them humble. If not, so many would play the higher ground card. If we are not careful, our problems can become our addiction.

CHAPTER XXII: God wants to heal you wherever you hurt

The Lord wants you to know that if you have a lingering, deep-seated disorder, it does not have to be the focal point of your existence. Because Dr Jesus is in the house, I repeat He wants to heal you everywhere you are ailing. You just have to cooperate with Him, He will lead you to victory, one step at a time. Whatever the problem may be, God has promised to restore and repair your past and meet your needs. Facing up to the truth is key to unlocking the prison doors that have kept you in bondage. Jesus is the key to loosening the chains that have held you in captivity.

I believe that my character was birthed in the school of hard knocks. Just look at me - I am writing a book! When God has a plan for your life, just know that He is going to design your training according to your leaning, as He sees fit. Jesus Himself had to undergo rigorous training before and during His ministry, and He was cooperative and obedient to the end. Jesus gave His father a free hand in His life, and we should do the same.

To further emphasise my point, I am going to give some examples of biblical figures such as Joseph, David, Moses, Job, even Solomon; they all seemed to have made a turnaround. These men did it God's way and were blessed and prospered. They kept the faith even when they could not see the end results. They came out as gold. I am also going to give some examples of those who did it their way. Cain, King Saul, and in modern day Adolph Hitler, with the dire consequences that followed them.

Looking at Joseph's story told in Genesis 37-50), he went through betrayal, was thrown in a pit, then sold as slave, and later imprisoned. Through all of Joseph's trials, God kept using him. Even in prison, all his training led towards him becoming Prime Minister of Egypt, second only to the king. Not only did God use Joseph to save the Egyptians from famine and starvation; he also used him to save his own family including his brothers who sinned against him, so Joseph went 'from the Pit to the Palace'. God says that when we are obedient to His words, He will make even your enemies be at peace with us.

Another example is King David told in 1 Samuel:17. He was anointed as a shepherd boy and a very insignificant last son. No one would believe that God would choose him. His brothers were strong warriors, serving in King Saul's army. Yet when, the Philistine giant, Goliath, threatened the Israel Army, God did not use any of them because they were all afraid to accept the challenge. In the absent of faith, there is only fear. But David wasn't afraid because he knew he had God on his side. Even though everyone laughed at such an unbelievable prospect, including the giant, David wasn't fazed. He prayed for strength and victory, then picked up is slingshot, carefully aimed and fired. Immediately, the giant fell, and David gave thanks to God. Without God's intervention in our lives, we cannot slay our giants. And we all have giants to defeat.

When God promises to do something great in our lives, it is not going to just come immediately; it will take time. During that time, He will strengthen us, and prepare us to operate in our calling. When David was anointed as King, he was just a young boy. After years of being persecuted and perused by King Saul, David had many moments of despair, and fear for his life. He had to hide out in caves, and other rough places, but God kept him. And He will keep you too. In order to change me, God took me far out of my comfort zone, but it had the desired effect. He pulled me apart and turned my life upside down to put me back together piece by piece. You see, when you are in God's waiting room, sometimes you need to be long-suffering, because you have to dig deep to find treasure. After all, grapes must be crushed to make wine, diamonds are carved out of carbon under pressure, olives are pressed to release oil, and likewise, seeds grow in darkness. So, whenever you feel crushed, under pressure, or in despair, you are in a powerful place of transformation and transmutation. Trust the process; you are God's diamond in the rough.

Even after David became King, he still had enemies, so he continued to trust God, to keep the crown on his head, as there were many challengers to his throne. Even when we get out breakthroughs, we still need God to keep us humble, and prayerful. So, no matter how long God's promise takes to be fulfilled in your life, wait on Him, and trust the process. He will renew your strength daily. When we rush God, we put

Him in a box, and limit His power to act in our lives. God did not promise to keep troubles from our door, nor did He say, we would not face struggles and hardships. He also did not promise that our Christian walk would be a bed of roses. We all have to carry our individual cross. What He did promise, however, is to take us through. The Bible is full of many examples of God's promises fulfilled in the lives of His saints.

For you to be proficient in any profession in life, you must be trained. The Word says to study to show yourself approved, unto God, as a workman that needed not to be ashamed, rightly dividing the word of truth (2 Timothy 2:1). A workman cannot work without knowledge of the job or task at hand, or without proper tools. Whether you receive your training in school, college, university, or any form of education, or even by just being well-read on the subject matter or the Bible, is essential.

Even a person who cannot read, they will be able to understand the word of God, but the wisdom of God is foolishness to the wisdom of this world and vice versa. God uses the foolish things of this world to confound the wise (1 Corinthians 3:19).

When you know the truth, it will set you free, and knowledge is power. Remember that lies only serve to keep us in bondage; even small lies can snowball into significant ones.

Chapter XXIII: Examples obedience versus disobedience

Then there was Moses, a man of few words, who escaped death by being hidden in a basket. He entered the Pharaoh's palace as a place of refuge, and was adopted and educated into the home, and the idolatrous ways of the Egyptians. Throughout this time, God had His hand on the reins of Moses's life. Even when he committed murder, God still kept him so that one day He could use Moses to deliver His people from slavery. Moses grew up and was educated as one of Pharaoh's family members and top generals. Throughout history, God placed His people in strategic positions to bring about His programme for the salvation of mankind. God will deal with you if you veer off course, as Moses' story is told in the book of Exodus. "For everyone to whom much is given, from him much will be required" (Luke 12:48), which means God chastens even those He loves and calls favourites. Think of all the suffering that Job went through: he lost his livelihood, his children, his health, and even his wife was angry with him. She told him to curse

God and die. Yet, through all of the horrendous suffering, he held on to his faith and remained faithful to God. As a result, God rewarded him with far more than he had before.

As previously stated, I was very material, and that seemed to replace God in my life. Thanks God that He is now the centre of my life. Don't love your possessions more than God, because He is a jealous God. If you hold on to your possessions, God cannot bring you to your fullest potential, and therefore He can only use you partially or not at all. Always remember that if God takes you to a situation, He will take you through it; you need to trust, obey, and let God work in His way. Don't bottle up your emotions; release them before they become cancerous. Every day, God is moulding and reshaping our character, as the potter moulds clay. So you had better sit back and enjoy the ride.

Let the word of God renew your mind. My mind used to be full of negative thoughts. It was constantly working, even during sleep. However, it's up to you to decide what you allow to infiltrate. Without God's control, the human mind is worldly and boundless, often on a path of self-destruction. It constantly generates thoughts, plans, schemes, and plots. It thirsts for knowledge, aiming to be a high achiever so it can be elevated and even worshipped. Sometimes, highly educated individuals develop delusions of grandeur, thinking they are more significant than they are and attempting to control everything.

However, without the restraining hand of God, power can corrupt. Absolute power corrupts absolutely. Consider how King Saul started out, promising to listen to and obey God. But later, he began to disobey and act according to his own will, until the spirit of the Lord left him, and he spiralled into a reprobate mind. You see, when a man makes promises, he often intends to keep them, but man's promise can only falter along the way, because of his disobedience and sinful nature. That's why we need God's hand in our lives to guide us and uphold us. David leaned on God consistently throughout his reign, and God remained faithful to him. David promised his best friend Jonathan, at his death, to take care of his remaining family members, and he did fulfil that promise.

We need to be open with God about our struggles because He already knows them. After all He made us. Jesus went through the same struggles when he was on earth and came out victorious. Therefore, He is the one who truly understands our weakness and has the solutions. King David was a man after God's own heart, not because he was perfect, or sinless, but because he was constantly on his knees in the throne room asking God to have mercy on him. Even when he took his eyes off God, and he messed up, by committing adultery and murder, and did not own it for a year, God still sent his prophet to warn him, to give him the opportunity to repent, because God knew that David would do just that. He knew David's heart. However, don't think that David did not suffer the consequences of his action, because the sword never left David's reign. Even his very household was full with controversy and betrayal. Even when David was told that he was not going to build God' dwelling place, but that his son Solomon was, David still humbled himself before God in a child-like manner. David lived in a constant throw of worship.

David's examples prove that "you can't hide it from God" (Hebrews 4:13-15). Likewise, Cane who killed his brother and buried his body in the ground, thinking that he had got away with murder. God made him accountable, like a lot of us today, who still think that we can hide our dastardly deeds from God, and never for a moment think God is watching.

The Bible says, "if riches increase, set not your heart upon them" (Psalms 62:10). Look at Solomon, who initially started out good and obedient, and God allowed him to build his dwelling place, which He had previously denied to his father David. All Solomon asked God for was wisdom, and not only did God grant his request, but He also gave him riches in abundance, and his wisdom increased, and his fame spread far and wide (2 Samuel, 1 Kings and 2 Chronical). However, like many others in high office, with money and power, pride also arose. He became disobedient to God's word by worshiping other God's. Unlike his dad before him, Solomon did not always put God first, because he wanted to sample everything that his money could afford. He forgot God and he suffered the consequence of his action.

Sometimes, when you can afford anything you want, unless you completely surrender your finance to God, it can lead you in the wrong direction. Take Adam and Eve. God gave them everything for their comfort in the garden. But they still weren't satisfied, so they partook of what was forbidden, bringing sin into the world. By taking their eyes off God, they suffered the consequences, and they were kicked out of their Godly home for good.

Some of us believe that money can buy happiness, whenever they show their lives of the rich and famous. They always show themselves being happy with their wealth. However, that is sometimes far from the truth however. Some are constantly stressed about how to keep their money, which means they will be constantly worrying about becoming poor. In fact, some of them are still committing suicide at a higher rate than the poor. Because some of them make money and possession their god. When you have God, instead, you have everything.

Even Hitler started out with good intentions, or so it appears. Then power wealth, greed, corruption, destructive thoughts, infiltrated his mind. When we don't surrender our minds to God, we can allow harmful thoughts and information to filter through. A mind unchecked will allow you to wander in all sorts of directions that you have no business in, because the mind is unquenchable. Hitler put himself on a pedestal to be worshipped, and the more he got away with, the eviler he became. He felt that he was god-like, dishing out ethnic cleansing. One of the reasons he gave for his horrific crimes against the Jewish nation, was that they had to be punished for crucifying Christ, who he did not even believe in. Power corrupts. Absolute power corrupts.

About our children

Like myself as a child, some of our children and young adults are so vulnerable in our society today, and subject to abuse. The danger is that if they are not given the love, correct discipline, guidance, motivation, and encouragement, that they need to positively move forward in life, their growth is stunted. The Bible says to train up a child in the way he should grow and when he gets older, he will not depart from that training. If you bring them up to hate or discriminate, they will grow up to hate and discriminate; if you abuse them, they will act out and abuse others. Some of the youths today are so angry, stressed, hopeless and discouraged, that they are harming themselves and others, primarily through knife and gun crimes. Stemming from substance abuse, alcohol, social drugs, and anything that can get them high to numb the pain and the rejection they feel, some in the end join gangs that are detrimental to their wellbeing in order to belong, and in the end even commit suicide. I thank God that He had a hand on the reins of my life.

And I thank Him for taking me through the most trying times in my life, and sticking with me, no matter how many times I failed. Our young people badly need help; they need to be moulded, and mentored the right way. They need an intervention. They need something to channel their negative energy into a positive way, and someone to care enough to give them a helping hand. They most definitely need God.

CHAPTER XXIV: Advise to single women starts here

Single people should wait on the Lord for their spouse. God has to prepare you for marriage. If single people, especially single women, would only wait on God to send them a partner, they would save themselves a lot of hurt down the line. I know that life can sometimes be lonely, not having that special someone to share it with. But if you know you cannot choose wisely for yourselves then allow God to choose for you, because He made you, so He has a mate that is tailor-made for you. God doesn't make mistakes, we do. Man sees the outward appearance, but God sees the heart. Wait on the Lord and trust in his judgment. However, for me, and perhaps some of you, God knew the partner I was going to choose from the very beginning, so He put His plan of action in place to help me through. Nothing and no one was going to stop God's plan for my life. Believe me, many tried along the way, without avail.

The reason I dedicated this section to single women is that I was one myself and made those same mistakes that some of you made and are going to make, and I have endured through my suffering. So, I hope that my experiences will go some way to make life a little more bearable and encourage you to wait on the Lord rather than endure years of unnecessary suffering down the line with the wrong partner. Because when the honey goes out of the moon, you are left with a honey-less moon - pardon the pun.

When single women listen to God, He will show them clear signs about their life partner. Your life partner needs to be your best friend and soulmate; he should be encouraging and supportive and be happy when you excel. God uses our struggles to effect change and growth in us. If your partner contributes to your spiritual growth and maturity, and is comforting you and lifting you up, when you are down, he is right for you. If you are the one doing all of the encouraging and the building up, to the detriment of yourself, that person is the wrong fit for you. Save yourself some hurt down the line because I assure you that, when the newness of the relationship fizzles out, you are both confronted with a stranger.

Wait on the Lord; He alone knows who is right for you and what is going to happen in your future. However, although you may choose the wrong partner, God will still restore, heal, and give you the grace to endure, but the process will cause you more pain than staying single. Put your trust in Him and allow Him to fulfil His promise in your life.

Although opposites attract, it doesn't always last. Make sure that you are truly hearing from God. You need to be compatible with your spouse, or marry in haste, repent at leisure. It means one, or both of you, will suffer in the relationship, your marriage will be broken, and if there are children involved, they will also suffer the consequences of your actions. Some of us rush into marriage for one reason or another because we can't wait on God; we just go our own way. We base our choice primarily on outward appearance, and then we expect God to sanction our union, by wrongly claiming that God chose our spouse. But when we believe wrongly, we act wrongly. And when further down the line, our marriage gets in trouble, now we call upon the Lord for help. And when He doesn't answer us straight away, we blame Him for giving us the wrong mate. Like when Adam and Eve sinned, they played the blame game. Eve said it was the serpent, and Adam said it was the woman given to him, both blaming God. (Genesis 2:21-22). Instead of taking responsibility for our own misjudgements, we apportion blame. So, when we mess up, we expect God to get us out of the mess we created in quick time. God is not saying no. He's saying He will fix you in his own time. However, if you really think you can choose your own partner, then do your own due diligence, check out his family, who his friends are, what job he does, if he has integrity, if he is a man of his word, whether he keeps his promise. Don't let him rush you, because if he rushes you into a relationship, he probably has something to hide, perhaps his true personality. No-one can keep up pretence for long; you need to play the long game because your happiness may depend on it.

Some wounds run deep, depending on how damaged we are in the relationship. God can heal us, but He has to get to the root of the matter. This could be many years of long-suffering. But if you have the faith to believe that God will restore your relationship better than before, then He will fulfil the desires of your heart (Psalms 37:4). So, we need to be patient and wait on the Lord. Sadly, many marriages end in divorce because of our impatience, and lack of knowledge. But did you know that God can still bring you back together even after a divorce? If you're still in love while separated and both want to reconcile, God can work on you individually, remoulding and reshaping you, and then put you back together, beautifully broken and submissive, ready to make the necessary changes for a marriage truly made in heaven. Another facet of marriage is when neither party is prepared to do what is necessary to get back on track. In cases of abuse in the relationship, where there is so much hurt involved, sometimes separation becomes the only viable option.

God made us to be in relationships with each other. When He created Adam, He saw that even with all He had given to Adam, he was still lonely. Note that God did not parade a selection of women in front of Adam and tell him to choose one; He tailor-made Eve for Adam, as told in Genesis. So, God said, "It is not good for man to be alone", and so He gave the first man his first lady to share his life with. God doesn't want you to be lonely; He wants us to live a happy and productive life. But some of us jump the gun because we can't wait for God's timing. Most of us who have lived life carry old baggage from past relationships into new ones. The Bible states, "no one puts new wine into old wineskins" (Mark 2:22). If you do. before long, cracks begin to emerge, suspicions arise, and trust falters.

First, God has to prepare us for marriage. He knows when we are ready, then He finds us someone compatible. someone both similar and different at the same time. Usually, it's someone as imperfect as us, so that He can work on us together. Remember, He will not give you someone to be your rock, because He is the only rock. So, wait on the Lord, and He will renew your strength.

I know it's easier said than done; waiting can be a lonely and frustrating process. God wants you to look to Him for help with your loneliness. He tells husbands to take care of married women, and He will take care of the single woman. He says, "Look to me; I will protect you, heal you, strengthen you, mend your broken heart, and restore all that the devil stole from you" (paraphrased from Psalm 34:18). He will guide you with His eye (Psalm 32:8). So, single women, don't waste your preciousness on worthless suitors with wrong agendas. Believe me, there is someone for everyone; you just need to let go, and God will send you your ideal mate. But I repeat, it will be in His timing. He will work on you until you don't need a husband, and then He will give you one. Remember, He wants you to rely on Him, not man, because God is a jealous God; man will always disappoint us, but when we rely on God, we won't be disappointed.

I remember reaching a stage in my life when I became cynical about marriage. I thought that if single people only knew how hard it can be to be married, they would prefer to stay single and wait on God. Singleness has so much freedom and less stress, without having two different personalities in the same space trying to navigate their way around each other's issues. But having said that, we all at times need someone to be accountable to, and God uses people for that purpose, so just breathe.

It is hard to admit, but it is true. Although God made some of us to be single, He gives us His grace to be content in our singleness. If your spouse has died, some may remarry, but those who can't, ask for more grace to endure. As I said before, God said that if you put Him first, all these things that you want shall be added unto you. In other words, He will give you the desires of your heart. Human beings cannot fill the gap in your heart; that space belongs to God. God made you for His glory, and if you search the world for eternity long, you will never find anyone like Him. Only God alone deserves the glory. Amen. Remember, even if God gives you a husband, things can still go wrong, because human beings are not perfect. Only God is perfect, and marriage takes hard work on both sides, and if you don't put the work in, things will go wrong, because God is putting two imperfect people together. You get out of a relationship what you put into it. So don't blame God like Adam and Eve did, put the work in, and watch God go to work in your marriage.

CHAPTER XXV: What others say about women and their relationships

Dr Faraah-Gray says: "The woman with the biggest heart attracts the men with broken souls". The doctor goes on to say that strong women scare weak men. I believe that weak men see this as a challenge and try to break down strong women. Weak men resort to name-calling and put downs, leading to heartbreak.

He continues to say: "Ladies, please understand that many times the only thing you did wrong was stay too long in a dead-end relationship. While there is a man putting you last, there is a king waiting to put you first. A woman becomes ten times the woman she is when she is loved correctly. Many women have lost countless good years staying loyal to toxic men. Ladies, you can't fix them; only God can."

Dating the wrong man at the expense of your happiness and peace is like setting your heart on fire to keep them warm. So, stop dating and feeling obligated to be with guys who aren't ready for you. You are the whole package, just delivered to the wrong address.

So, single women, make sure your own life is right before you become somebody else's wife. You don't need a man to complete you; only God can complete you. Stop saying, "I need a man to take care of me and help me through this". God is your helper; He is just waiting for you to acknowledge Him.

Some of you might be wondering why I haven't pushed myself forward before this. The answer is that God has been working on me behind the scenes. He has kept me in the background while working on my character and issues. We must allow the Master Builder to do His best work in us. I believe that there are two types of people: those who keep it in, and sometimes bottle up their issues, then explode when they can't keep it in anymore, and those without filter and have to let it out whatever the cost. God wants us to be somewhere in the middle; we need to strike a balance. Jamaicans have a saying, "Sticks and stones may break my bones, but words will never hurt me." That is so not true. Words can cause deep wounds from which some of us may never recover. The tongue is a sharp weapon without a shield. Let's be clear, I was lashed with both the tongue and whip. Yes, I was used and abused, but I will never let that define me. However, true words spoken with love can bring healing. The Bible says, "faithful are the wounds of a friend" (Proverbs 27:8). And know this: we have to watch our tongue; speak words that heal, and not words that wound. The Bible says "death and life are in the power of the tongue, and they that love it shall eat of its fruits" (Proverbs 18:21).

After coming out of captivity, God told the Israelites that they would eat bitter herbs. Why? As a reminder of the bitterness they experienced in Egypt, under the rule of Pharaoh, and be grateful to God for his Deliverance. Stay humble, and do not grow and become bitter, as a result of their years of bondage. How does bitterness start? It results from the offenses people commit against us and that we don't let go of. The things we regurgitate over and over until they become blown out of proportion. They become the bedrock of our very existence. The longer we allow them to grow and fester, the deeper-rooted and embedded they become. But know this: a root of bitterness left unchecked will infect our very being, our attitude, behaviour, perspective, and relationships, especially with God. So, exercise foresight by looking carefully, so that no one falls short of God's grace, and that no root of bitterness springs up to cause trouble, as by this many become defiled or corrupted (Hebrews 12:15).

In reality, life is a series of tests, of which we either pass or fail. But even in our failures, we can still triumph if we never give up. In other words, it's not just about how you start, but how you finish. The word says, "O Lord of hosts, who judges rightly and justly, who tests the hearts and the mind [..]. to you, I have revealed my cause" (Jeremiah 11:20).

You see, all of our lives are filled with challenges. Tests examine our resolve, determination, and character. These tests are meant to strengthen us and bring us into a deeper and closer relationship with God. They help us to truly know ourselves while identifying any major flaws in our character. God's tests are for both His benefit and ours. He tests us by applying pressure, to our lives to see if we can withstand and respond in a godly way. He does this to highlight our strengths and weaknesses, so that we can achieve our goals by playing to our strengths. In other words, God applies pressure so that we can reach our goal, which should always be to pass, not avoid. In reality, tests often come before promotion. So, if you want promotion, you will have to take and pass a test. When God tests us, growth will follow. God will continue to highlight the areas He needs to work on in us. With our cooperation, we must comply if we want God's best in our lives.

CHAPTER XXVI: Life today

I look at my life today. I thank God for being in it. I remember a number of years ago, when I was having a conversation about my entry into Christianity with a family member named Stella, who was very supportive of me at a time when I really needed it. I will always be grateful to her. When I told her about the time I got saved, she was so surprised and said she thought I was always a Christian.

So I thought, wow, my decision to fight bad with good was working then. That is how I tried to live my life. This made me think about how long I have known and loved the Lord. from an early age, the first time I was shown the illustrated Bible. Even before I could read, I knew Jesus and fell in love with Him. And through my love for Him, He opened up to me with the stories in the Bible which have helped navigate my way through life's hard knocks. I am glad that Stella saw what I was trying so hard to achieve in my life. Because I have always strived to treat people the way I want to be treated, but the execution of that can be hard to maintain, without God. It is impossible to be good without Christ, because this world is built upon turning good into bad, leading to unrighteousness, and deceit. The world thinks that they can be good in their own strength, but they are deceived. The devil has them right where he wants them, knowing exactly what buttons to push to expose all that false goodness. Even Jesus never claimed to be good. When He was called a good master, He said, "Why do you call me good? No one is truly good except God alone" (Mark 10:18). The only people who concern God are the ones who enter into a personal relationship with Jesus, their Saviour, and Him.

It was due to my faith in God's salvation and redemption, that I found it in my heart to forgive my stepdad, and at the same time, I ministered to him the salvation of Jesus Christ, around two-three weeks before his death. Through my journey, I am also happy that the Lord used me to minister Salvation to many people over the years, including family members, friends, and strangers. And long may it continue.

Additionally, and as previously stated, one of the positive outcomes of my learning curve was that

I was able to bring up my son in a Godly and positive way. With God's help, I am proud of the way he turned out. He met and married a good woman, in answer to my prayer. Now I have two beautiful grandchildren with my birth son, and I am even more blessed to have two stepsons which have given me five more grandchildren. I am happy to say that they are also doing well and have stable jobs. I trust God to keep them.

To reiterate, the message the Lord gave me is to tell my people you can't hide it from God. One good memory I have from life in Jamaica is when the Lord showed me a vision. He said there were two men working in the field, and one was jealous of the other's relationship with God. So, one killed the other and buried his body in the field, then looked around, making sure that no one saw him. It wasn't until I was in my forties that I asked God who the story was about. He told me it was Cain and Abel. The point of the story, He said, was that His people are doing so many wicked things behind closed doors, thinking that He cannot see them. So, He is giving me a Truth Ministry: "Tell my people that you can't hide it from God [...] Neither is there any creature that is not manifest in his sight: but all things are naked and opened unto the eyes of Him with whom we have to do" (Hebrews 4:13). Because God is an all-seeing, all-knowing, jealous God. "Can a man hide himself in hiding places, so I do not see him? 'Do I not fill the heavens and the earth?' declares the Lord" (Jeremiah 23:24).

But before I could fully realise my ministry, I had to tell my own truth.

CONCLUSION: A Memory Looking Back

I remember when I was out and about with my brothers and sisters. People would never believe it when they introduced me as their older sister. I would get responses like, "You don't look like them". That was when I literally felt like the black sheep of the family because I wasn't fair in complexion. I couldn't be related to them, and I got to the stage where I would introduce them as friends. I remember my sister Edna saying, "No, I am not her friend; she is my sister". I felt proud at that. They have never, to my knowledge, not acknowledged me as their older sister to outsiders, and to date, that has not changed. However, to insiders, I always felt left out. They would protect me from outsiders, but if I ever had any disagreements with one of them, they would stand together against me, rightly or wrongly.

My mom and my stepdad have now passed away. God rest their souls. Dad passed away over twenty years before mom, who passed in 2017, still resentful and raw, from passed hurt. I pray that God gave her the peace she needed, before she passed. Mom had always dreamed of returning to Jamaica, even though Dad was not so keen. When Dad passed away, mom called us all to gather and told us of her decision to go back home to Jamaica. We saw that it was her heart's desire, so we gave her our blessing. In Jamaica, mom lived comfortably for possibly seventeen-eighteen years. We all contributed in our own ways to help make mum as comfortable as possible, according to our abilities, and those who were in better financial positions were able to contribute more.

Sadly, as Mom approached her twilight years, she began to have mental health issues. As long as we only talked about certain aspects of the past, we were fine. I realised that she couldn't handle anything too distressing, or even remember most things anyway. I just worked at her pace and continued to enjoy watching the same old movies she loved, but the best and happiest times I had with my mom were when we went shopping alone together.

I miss and love her dearly. I came to understand that mom had many unresolved issues from her own past. That's why, when in the past, I tried to talk about my own issues, she would say, "Well, I went through a lot too, you know". However, I still ache for the relationship I never had with my mom. The contents of this book are not new; I spoke about them while mom and dad were alive, forgave them, and asked for their forgiveness for my part in our disagreements. None of us are perfect; we all make mistakes. It's how we handle ourselves and learn from our mistakes that sets us apart. So, I am revealing this now as part of my healing process.

I'm aware that many people, both adults and children, have suffered like I have, and possibly worse, and are still suffering. My advice to you is to tell the truth, even if no one believes you. Turn it over to Jesus. He answers all prayers and will put the right people and circumstances in place to help you. The damage only occurs if you keep it to yourself. So, don't suffer in silence; speak out. When you know and tell the truth, the truth will set you free. God will never give you more than you can bear (John 8:32). The Bible says, "when your father and mother forsake you, the Lord will take care of all that concerns you" (Psalm 27:10). In my life, telling the truth has certainly brought me healing, however painful.

Loving Sister Daniela

I remember being so insecure and desperate for validation, always comparing myself to others, especially my sister Edna. One day I asked my younger sister, Daniela, "Who do you think is prettier, me or Edna?". Her reply was, bless her heart, "I love both my sisters!". How could it be otherwise? However, the fact was that Edna and I were always arguing with each other. She was usually in the wrong, and when I, as the older sister, tried to correct her, she would refuse to listen. So, I would complain to mom. Edna would deny it, and mom would believe her over me without fail. But I remember being about twelve and I went into the lodger's kitchen and took a piece of meat from her pot. This time I was defiantly in the wrong. That wasn't something I usually did, so I was nervous. Of course, Edna caught me. "Angela, what are you doing?", she asked, fully aware of what I had done. "Nothing!" I said, and she immediately went to tell mom. I rushed to flush the meat down the toilet. This time, mom was right to scold me, I was so embarrassed.

I want to pause here and talk a bit about my sister Daniela. She was the youngest girl, and we were very close. We were always around each other. With her, I felt like the older sister because she cared about what I had to say, and I felt her love. That was refreshing. She was a pretty little thing, fair in complexion and very slim. When it came to my stepdad, she seemed to be his least favoured. Just seeing her would set him off, and he would verbally abuse her, calling her all sorts of negative names. She would just take it, rocking forwards and backwards in the sofa. I hated it and felt so sorry for her, but I was too young to do anything. I would simply give her love. As time passed, after I left home, the older boys also began to verbally abuse Daniela, following in their dad's footsteps. To this day, I haven't seen any changes. I always say children live by what they learn. The Bible says, "train up a child in the way he should go, and when he is old, he will not depart from it." (Proverbs 22:6). After I left home and returned for a visit, I found a changed Daniela. She was mouthy, angry, and sarcastic, putting people down to get attention and always on the defensive. I was so shocked by the change in Daniela. I asked her, "Daniela, what happened to you?". One of the things she said was, "Why did you leave me?". All I could say was, "I had to leave for my own sanity". What more could I say?

I felt sadness for the change in her character, but I also felt the resentment she had for me leaving her. However, this is my version of events. I won't speak anymore for her; I'm sure she has her own story to tell, or not.

So, back to my story. Like myself, mom also had a difficult relationship with food, and her weight would fluctuate. It was through food that she showed her love. As for me, I know that I had many negative emotions attached to food; I saw food as either a reward or punishment, which was quite messed up. My son once told me, "Mom, you seem to have a love-hate relationship with food. You need to see a nutritionist". So, clearly my eating disorder began with Bernese back in Jamaica. As a child, one of the punishments she imposed on me was starvation one minute and overfeeding me the next. She would cook a whole pot of cornmeal, make it thick, then force me to eat all of it until my stomach was bursting, so I perceived that mum and I ate emotionally.

Importantly, this is why I believe my message is crucial for our well-being. A big part of this is your diet. God made food for our enjoyment, but the devil attached guilt and other negative connotations to it. Do you know that the Lord once referred to me as a 'fat woman' and I did not like it one bit? I was so upset, and I wondered if this is how He saw me. I thought I was going to lose this weight and show Him. All because I attached so many negative attachments to being fat. Similarly, some of us eat through our feelings, and that is hardly satisfying. It takes a lot of energy to hold onto negative emotions, and no one is worth the energy it takes to hate them. The Lord has shown me this over many years. In my experience, the fears we carry from the past often lie in the experiences we had back then. The only way to change them is to tackle them head-on. Clearly, forgiveness is the best tonic for heart ailment, and the only way to truly move forward. If you don't forgive, you'll be forever stuck in a time capsule, repeating the same mistakes. The Bible says, "If we confess our sins, He is faithful and just to forgive us and cleanse us from all unrighteousness." (1 John 1:9).

I took a trip to Jamaica on April 20th, 2018, where I wrote the bulk of my book, sitting on my lovely veranda, sipping some lovely coconut water, trusting God to help me write what comes next.

In writing this book, every day I felt that I was drawing closer to God, while seeing His promises fulfilled in my life. Each day I woke up, I thanked Him for blowing breath in my body, and the same for my loved ones. So, although my life has come full circle, I've gone through testing and turbulent times through my childhood, my relationships, and my marriage. I decided not to give up on my marriage. So, we tried to address our issues through counselling, but I used to get so frustrated with my husband because I'm open about our problems, because I want us to be healed, whereas he only shares what he wants to share with the counsellor. I keep telling him that the councillor is not our friend; she is there to help us save our marriage. So instead of telling the truth he ends up attacking me on what I say, so we end up more distant. We need to be transparent about our issues, it is essential to mend what is broken. Now, we are a work in progress, and by God's grace, we are heading in the right direction. We are in a better place today.

As I sit back and wonder how I'm going to finish my story, looking back at my life's journey, I can only thank God for His goodness, mercy, and grace. His mercy kept me so I wouldn't let go. If it weren't for the Lord who was on our side, where would we be? Throughout my life, the Lord has always put someone in place to bring me His message. Whether I listened or not, I'm grateful that I eventually got the message. God kept showering me with His grace.

What's imperative in this life is that forgiveness is a gift that keeps on giving. It's a gift you give to yourself repeatedly. When you keep forgiving yourself, you become stronger and more compassionate towards others. So, no more will I drink the poison of unforgiveness. The Bible rightly says, "to whom you forgive anything, I forgive also. For if I forgive anything, I forgive it for your sake" (2 Corinthians 2:10). Additionally, "God's Word clearly says that when we don't forgive, we are undiscerning, unloving, unmerciful, and untrustworthy" (Romans 1:31). I know that it's easier said than done because when you've been hurt, it's easier to put up barriers. But we must be careful because a protective exterior can turn your heart to stone and distance you from God. One Christian author writes that the only thing more painful, and carries serious ramifications, than a broken heart is a frozen heart. So, you just have to let it go and let God in. A soft heart is not a weak or naive one. On the contrary, wisdom, experience, and faith seasoned with mercy make for a strong heart" (paraphrased from Gass, 2024). For me, I'd rather have a soft heart wrapped in faith, dripping with mercy, love, and obedience to God any day, than go back to where I have been, forever lost. Thank you, Lord.

I cannot emphasise more, that you take God's warning seriously, because "You can't hide anything from God" (Hebrews 4:13-15), no matter how cleaver you think you are.

Cain couldn't hide his brother's murder.

Joseph's brothers couldn't hide the fact that they sold him into slavery.

David couldn't hide his adultery with Bathsheba, and the murder of her husband Uriah.

Moses couldn't hide the murder of the Egyptian.

Job couldn't escape his trial by fire.

Hitler couldn't wipe out the Jewish Nation.

So why don't you just trust and believe that God will clean up your mess, and use you as a diamond in the rough, for His Glory. The Gospel song, 'The Goodness of God'; is appropriate here because it is a testament to his constant love and goodness in my life:

I love you Lord for your mercies never fails me, all my days I have been held in your hand, from the moment that I wake up until I lay my head I will sing of the Goodness of God, for all my life you have been faithful, for all my life you have been so, so Good, with every breath I am able, I will sing of the Goodness of God, I will sing of the Goodness of God, your Goodness is running after me, your goodness is running after me... readers when you have experience God's Goodness, there is no turning back, and I will never turn back.

Why? As I said before, God is all-seeing, all-knowing, all-powerful, all-consuming, and cannot lie.

THE END

Acknowledgments

First and foremost, I give the uttermost thanks to my Lord and Saviour Jesus Christ, Father, Son and Holy Ghost, for being my everything, and for walking me through life's journey, leading me every step of the way. Thank you for inspiring and helping me to write this book.

My son Sean for his unconditional love, his uplifting words, and constant support throughout the years. He certainly has a wise head on your shoulders. He is a true inspiration to me and all those around him. Son, I am so proud of you and what you have accomplished. I thank God for you every day. Love you lots.

Mercedes, I thank you for being the best wife my son could ask for. Yours is truly a marriage made in heaven. I know that my grandchildren are safe in your hands. I love you like my own flesh and blood.

To my granddaughters Shy and Leah, thank you for your love and support. Lots of love!

My dear friend Elizah for so much, that it is hard to put it into words. She came through for me when I was homeless and lost and alone, and she made a place in her home for me. She just took charge, when I was weak, and couldn't think clearly, she loaned me her strength. She helped me even in the face of opposition. I thank God for her every day. Thank you, dear friend, you will forever be in my heart.

My dear friend Sharon for her longstanding friendship, loyalty and always being there when I needed her. Thanks for always lending a listening ear, her gifts, her encouragement. She uplifts me so much in words and deeds. She is one of my biggest cheerleaders, and a special thanks for her presence at my graduation, and for always believing in me. Words just can't explain how much it means to me. Much love dear friend.

My dear Church sister and friend Kristy, for your love, loyalty, and support. For always lending a listening ear, and giving encouraging words. Most grateful thanks for giving me a platform to minister the Gospel.

Thanks, dear sister Daniela for your love and support.

To my dear friend Dorean. She stuck by me even when times were scary. She put herself in harm's way for me. Thank you for your love and loyalty, and for being there for the long haul

Dear Barbara, thanks for being my constant and loyal friend.

Thanks, Pastor Powell and Sis Alyne for their love and support. Sis Alyne, for her wise counselling. Pastor Powell for giving me my first platform, for his support in my ministry, his encouraging words, and for seeing more in me than I saw in myself.

An extra shout out to my lovely Wednesday prayer team. Thanks for your love, support, faithfulness, and obedience to God's word, and for listening to my messages faithfully each week. Love you guys.

Thanks to my husband for his love and support.

Bibliography

- The Bible New International Version (NIV), (n.d.), 1 Corinthians 7:32, 2 Corinthians 2:10, Exodus 34:14, Genesis 2:21-22, Hebrews 12:15, Hebrews 4:13-75, Hosea 4:6, James 4:8, Jeremiah 11:20, John 5:5-6, 1 John 1:9, John 8:32, Luke 6:46-49, Matthew 18:20- 21, Matthew 6:14-16, Psalm 27:10, Psalm 32:8, Psalm37:1, Psalm 42:11, Psalm 139:14, Psalm 145:5 ,1 Peter 5:7, Proverbs 18:21, Romans 1:31

- The Bible King James Version (KJV), (n.d.), 1 Corinthians 7:32, 2 Corinthians 2:10, Exodus 34:14, Genesis 2:21-22, Hebrews 12:15, Hebrews 4:13-75, Hosea 4:6, James 4:8, Jeremiah 11:20, John 5:5-6, 1 John 1:9, John 8:32, Luke 6:46-49, Matthew 18:20- 21, Matthew 6:14-16, Psalm 27:10, Psalm 32:8, Psalm37:1, Psalm 42:11, Psalm 139:14, Psalm 145:5 ,1 Peter 5:7, Proverbs 18:21, Romans 1:31

- The Bible English Standard Version (ESV), (n.d.), 1 Corinthians 7:32, 2 Corinthians 2:10, Exodus 34:14, Genesis 2:21-22, Hebrews 12:15, Hebrews 4:13-75, Hosea 4:6, James 4:8, Jeremiah 11:20, John 5:5-6, 1 John 1:9, John 8:32, Luke 6:46-49, Matthew 18:20- 21, Matthew 6:14-16, Psalm 27:10, Psalm 32:8,

Psalm37:1, Psalm 42:11, Psalm 139:14, Psalm 145:5 ,1 Peter 5:7, Proverbs 18:21, Romans 1:31

- Meyer J. (2015), Closer to God Each Day Devotional: 365 Devotions for Everyday Living, Hodder & Stoughton
- Gass B. and D, (2024), The Word for Today Daily Bible Devotional, available at: https://vision.org.au/the-word-for-today-reading/
- Elvis Presley (1970) 'The Wonder of You', On Stage [Vinyl], written by Baker Knight, New York: RCA Victor.

Printed in Great Britain
by Amazon